Positive Caregiving

Positive Caregiving

CARING FOR OLDER LOVED ONES
USING THE POWER *of* POSITIVE EMOTIONS

By

Sarah Teten Kanter, Ph.D.

THE
collective.
BOOK STUDIO

Library of Congress Cataloging-in-Publication Data available.

ISBN: 978-1-68555-953-3

Ebook ISBN: 978-1-68555-406-4

Library of Congress Control Number: 2022916019

Printed using Forest Stewardship Council certified stock
from sustainably managed forests.

Manufactured in China.

Design by Andrea Kelly.

Typesetting by Maureen Forys, Happenstance Type-O-Rama.

1 3 5 7 9 10 8 6 4 2

The Collective Book Studio®
Oakland, California
www.thecollectivebook.studio

For my son, Spencer, my never-ending
source of love and awe.

———————

Thank you first and foremost to editors Elizabeth Dougherty
and Kate Hanely for your guidance, expertise, and support
in writing this book. Thank you to my husband, Troy, for your
unwaivering belief in me and this mission and for always
encouraging me to be the best person I can be. Thanks to
my mom and dad for a lifetime of unconditional love, and
a special thank-you to all the caregivers out there—past,
present, and future—the world is better because of you.

Contents

Caregiving: From Obligation to Opportunity

If you are reading this, you are likely one of the 40-plus million unpaid caregivers caring for an older loved one in the United States. And like many nonprofessional caregivers, you were probably moving along through life, comfortable in your day-to-day routine, when suddenly everything changed. While caregiving is common, it's a different experience for everyone. It may be that you got a call from the hospital that your mom had fallen and broken a bone, or that your spouse had a heart attack. Perhaps you learned your dad was diagnosed with Alzheimer's disease or that your aunt was ready for hospice. You may be trying to manage care for a loved one who lives far away from you or who has moved into a care community. Maybe the person you're caring for already lives with you, or is moving in, and caregiving is now a daily part of your life. No matter how your caregiving story began, or what shape it takes, the outcome is the same: Your life story—and your loved one's life story—now contains a new chapter.

Although it may not feel this way in this moment, this chapter is definitively finite. While your caregiving role may last a few weeks, a few years, a decade, or more, it *will* end. The challenge—and the opportunity—is to make the most of this time.

I am not trying to brightside you: Caregiving can be difficult, stressful, and scary. It can induce feelings of sadness, intense worry, and anxiety. The person you are caring for probably knows exactly how to push your buttons. And yet, caring for a loved one can be one of the most rewarding roles you have in your lifetime. No matter how long or how short your caregiving experience lasts, you can choose to use this time to refocus your attention on what matters most in life. This book will help you do that.

The Positive Caregiving Approach

As a gerontologist, I have spent the past decade gaining a deeper understanding of how people change and evolve as they grow older. I have seen evidence that both caregiving and care receiving as we and our loved ones age can be extremely rewarding—a time of enrichment rather than depletion. My doctoral research focused specifically on the emotional experiences of people living with Alzheimer's disease. What I have learned is that *all* people, even those living with cognitive disorders, retain their ability to feel emotions as they age.

And I've seen that often the person who needs the most support in adjusting to their new reality isn't the person who is ill or adapting to new age-related changes—it's the caregiver. *But most importantly*, I have learned that positive emotions like gratitude, love, and awe, and all the things that induce them, are what make life worthwhile.

My research has led me to realize that caregiving offers a unique opportunity to recognize and reframe your own worldview, steep yourself (and your care partner) in positive emotions, foster your own growth and resilience through personal practices, and strengthen your bond to your care partner through reminiscing about times that have come before as well as savoring the present moment. I have combined these pillars into a framework I call Positive Caregiving, and in this book, I will walk you through exactly how to incorporate each of these pillars into your daily life, even with your additional caregiving duties.

Following the Positive Caregiving approach not only may reduce the stress of caregiving, but also can deliver numerous benefits, including:

- A *deeper bond with the person you're caring for,* even if your relationship was fraught to begin with.

- A *toolbox of skills* that helps you bring your best self to caregiving now, and that can enrich your life and your well-being into the future.

- *Mental and physical health support*—for yourself and the person you're caring for—as the positive emotions this book helps you harness have many powerful, research-supported health benefits.

- *A reconnection to what matters in life.* Of course, caregiving can be challenging, but it also can reorient your attention away from daily stressors that can so easily erode quality of life.

- *An increased sense of purpose.* Devoting time and energy to reducing someone else's suffering while helping them thrive is hard work, but it can also be an experience that bolsters your own strength and resilience.

To help you head into your caregiving journey with a more positive mindset, Part 1 of this book helps you understand the opportunities caregiving provides and reframes the narrative on caregiving—to begin to see it not as an inherent burden, but as a beginning. You'll learn about ways to open your mind to the possibilities of caregiving and how to tap into the tremendous power of positive emotions. Part 1 also translates the concepts behind Positive Caregiving into four "pillars" that can transform your life and relationships, along with the lives of those for whom you are caring:

- *Perspective*—accepting and embracing your worldview while using positive psychology to create new lenses for seeing and experiencing the world as a caregiver.

- *Savoring*—using techniques from mindfulness and meditation to become more present and more aware of your experiences of positive emotions.

- *Reminiscence*—reflecting and reviewing past experiences to help you and your care partner make meaning out of current circumstances and life in general.

- *Growth*—combining the principles of positive psychology and lifestyle medicine into personal practices that foster your own personal development even (especially!) during the daily realities of being a caregiver.

Part 2 of the book immerses you in five specific positive emotions—gratitude, empathy, forgiveness, love, and awe—that are central to caregiving relationships and that have been shown to improve health, reduce stress, and create meaning in daily life. Each chapter will help you understand the power of a specific emotion, and includes activities designed to help you experience that emotion. There are "shared activities" you can do with your care partner and "personal practices" you can do on your own. While the activities are of varying lengths, they all include:

- an intentional "lens" of a positive emotion to frame or reframe the day

- a bit of historical wisdom to set the tone

- an activity to share with your loved one

- a personal practice you can do on your own as part of self-care.

For the vast majority of us, giving and receiving care is inevitable—not an *if*, but a *when*. I encourage you to use this unique time with your loved one to refuel your senses of purpose, wonder, and gratitude. To take an approach to the experience that can make you feel more alive, hopeful, energetic, and brimming with well-being. The first step often is just a matter of realizing that a different experience of caregiving is possible, and then getting a little guidance and support on how to savor, rather than endure, this time. That realization, information, and encouragement is what I hope this book will provide, and that the activities I've included will help transform what can be a challenging experience into a rewarding one.

Being alive, after all, is a momentary phenomenon. Caregiving for others—and especially for our loved ones—reminds us of this reality and provides us with the opportunity to appreciate each and every day. So, let's get started. There's no time like right now to savor the present.

—Sarah Teten Kanter, PhD

PART 1

Reframing the Caregiving Experience

"Love is a flower that grows
in any soil, works its sweet
miracles undaunted by autumn
frost or winter snow, blooming
fair and fragrant all the year,
and blessing those who give
and those who receive."

—Louisa May Alcott (1832–1888)

Chapter 1

Caregiving as an Invitation to Grow

As I was walking into the entrance of a local retail store, I saw my friend Portia. We hadn't connected in several months, and I was excited to see her. But my excitement quickly turned to concern as she relayed that her mother-in-law had recently fallen in the parking lot of a grocery store. (I live in Nebraska, where it is often icy in the winter and spring.)

I listened to Portia talk about how disruptive and tense it had been for her and her husband to figure out where his mother should recuperate, and how to make sure she was getting all the care that she needed. As a gerontologist, I am used to having these conversations. I often get frantic phone calls from friends (and from friends of friends) who are navigating the way reality changes when an older relative gets hurt or becomes ill.

I always validate these friends' stress, because it's real. When someone suddenly finds themselves in a caregiving role, it's generally because someone they love is ill, injured, or frail, all of which can cause justifiable feelings of fear, sadness, and anxiety. But I also always point out the positive opportunities that are inherent in caregiving—as an invitation to reflect on what matters most, a chance to build deeper connections with their loved one while there is still time, and an opportunity to enrich their lives deeply.

When I talked to Portia about caregiving from a positive perspective that day in the store entrance, I could see her shoulders lowering and hear her voice losing its anxious tone. "Talking to you is making me feel a lot better about all of this," she confessed.

It wasn't me who brought that relief—it was Portia's realization that caring for her mother-in-law was an important and meaningful opportunity rather than a problem to be solved. The same is true for any of us who find ourselves thrust into a caregiving role.

Because of recent changes in human history, we are all practically guaranteed to become either a caregiver or a care recipient, or both. The sooner we find our way to accept this invitation, the sooner we can suffer less and savor more.

Caregiving as a Fact of Life

According to the U.S. Census Bureau, from 1960 to 1990, the number of people over the age of 65 in the United States doubled from around 16 million to 32 million. It is projected to more than double again to over 70 million by 2030, when this segment of the population is expected to surpass one billion worldwide. The increase in the United States is due in large part to the fact that during the last century, the average lifespan of Americans has risen from around 60 to 80. Of course, this increase in human longevity is something to be celebrated and revered. But there's a flip side: We now have a significantly longer experience of aging. As we live longer, and as more of our population comprises those 65 and older, our cultural and social understanding of the human experience needs to change, too.

Of course, being older does not equate to being frail or even needing significant help with activities of daily living. Despite popular belief, the majority of older adults in the United States maintain their independence and remain in their own homes or their chosen community their entire lives—especially with the help of loved ones, paid caregivers, and in-home care services. And there have been major innovations in how we provide care for the small percentage (less than 10 percent)[1] of those who need some type of long-term care. Assisted living communities (which were first created in the 1980s) and living platforms like continuing care retirement communities (CCRCs) that provide for progressive care needs as people age are examples of solutions for meeting the needs of our diverse aging population. Yet more than 40 million people—mostly relatives, primarily female, and largely over the age of 50 themselves—continue to find their life roles altered and broadened as they become an informal caregiver (also known as an unpaid caregiver) due to a loved one's changing health, illness, or recovery.

According to AARP, informal caregivers spend on average a little more than 20 hours per week helping their care recipients, performing tasks that include everything from washing clothes, cooking, and shopping to administering medicine, attending doctors' appointments, and managing insurance claims. This informal caregiving accounts for more than 990 million hours of care a year. *Think about all that love.*

In survey after survey, aging Americans overwhelmingly indicate that they want to "age in place," remain independent, and "don't want to be a burden" to family and friends.

The devotion to self-reliance in America has subsequently bolstered the negative narratives around caregiving. And there has been plenty of gerontological research focused on supporting this narrative.[2] The majority of caregiving research has been focused on the associations between caregiving and negative physical and psychological outcomes,[3] such as depression, stress, anxiety, fatigue, overwhelming feelings, and obesity. More than 100 scales have been created for researchers to use to assess the impact of caregiving of older adults, but less than a third of them are focused on measuring the positive effects of caregiving.[4] One study from the 1980s coined the term "caregiver burden," leading to hundreds more studies examining how caregivers assess their own "burden."[5] A second seminal study, which was focused on spousal caregivers of heart patients, found that caregiving was a risk for mortality and it has now been cited thousands of times as evidence that caregiving is detrimental to one's health.[6] Many of these studies have been focused on small numbers of subjects, were based on convenience sampling, which may skew the results, or focused solely on dementia caregivers, whose experience cannot be generalized to all caregivers. Yet they continue to drive this story line that caregiving is overwhelming and harmful to one's physical and mental well-being. With phrases such as "caregiver burnout," "the sandwich generation," and "already toast" becoming part of our daily language, caregiving is most often painted as a burden to be borne, rather than the beneficial experience that it can be.

Evidence Supports a Different Narrative

While some negative effects of caregiving can't be denied, not all caregivers experience the adverse outcomes so frequently attributed to caregiving. In fact, more recent population-based research studies have painted a quite different, more positive picture of the caregiving experience.[7] These studies highlight that for most people, the positives associated with caregiving, such as deepened relationships with loved ones and a strengthened sense of purpose, outweigh the negatives.[8] Multiple studies have also found that caregivers actually have increased longevity and well-being compared to their non-caregiver counterparts—even among those with their own chronic health problems or poor mental health[9]—and that the positive aspects of caregiving can mitigate negative effects that may arise.[10]

How then can you move the needle on your caregiving experience toward the positive more than the negative? There are many small acts that can help counteract some of the potential challenges associated with caregiving. Simply approaching caregiving with a positive outlook and thinking of it as the opportunity that it can be is a good first step.

When called to care, most people step up out of love and compassion. Using that love and compassion, as well as other positive emotions, to fuel your caregiving efforts is another step toward what can be a significant personal growth experience.

Best of all, this reframing and these positive emotions are free, and easy to access for everyone—no matter your personal history, level of busyness, or income.

Choosing to view caregiving as a positive experience presents one of the most pivotal possibilities of our lifetime and for the future of humanity. Imagine a world where:

- Aging is synonymous with the opportunity to experience cherished things in life.

- Caring for aging loved ones is a role that is anticipated, revered, and regarded as a rite of passage in our adult development.

- Caregiving is viewed as a critical role for all genders, and this work is valued both individually and collectively as one of the most important aspects of life.

Let's explore how this vision is not only possible but also can become a reality that is available to anyone who wants to be a part of it.

- As we live longer, the potential need for care-giving rises along with our life expectancy.

- Societal influences, such as having a high regard for independence, influence how we view caregiving.

- A large portion of research that looks at the effects of caregiving on caregivers is focused on the negative.

- Despite this societal and scientific bias, there are many research-backed benefits of caregiving—they just aren't talked about. These benefits include increased longevity and sense of purpose.

- Caregiving can be a meaningful and enriching experience.

> *"The highest reward for a person's toil is not what they get for it, but what they become by it."*
>
> —John Ruskin (1819–1900)

Chapter 2

The Pillars of Positive Caregiving

Will there be stress, frustration, exhaustion, and sadness at times along your caregiving journey? I can almost guarantee it. But isn't that part of life in general? A mix of good and bad days? And a blend of positive and negative emotions within the course of the same day—and sometimes even in the same moment? As humans we often seek to soothe and shelter ourselves from life's more challenging experiences. The paradox is that many of these difficult experiences ultimately can lead to our most significant growth and serve as our most effective routes to discovering meaning and purpose.

Positive Caregiving offers a path for people who want to make the most of their caregiving experience. It does so through a combination of disciplines, philosophies, and strategies that have well-established track records of helping people deal with challenges that are intrinsic to being human. Some have existed for millennia, and others have been developed in the last few decades. They include positive psychology, lifestyle medicine, reminiscence therapy, meditation, and mindfulness.

- *Positive psychology:* Positive psychology is the scientific study of what psychological factors, such as personality traits, emotions, and behaviors, allow and encourage humans to thrive. The term was coined in 1998 by Martin Seligman, PhD, then the president of the American Psychological Association.[11]

- *Lifestyle medicine:* Lifestyle medicine, formally named in 1989, encourages and even prescribes lifestyle actions, such as sleep, a healthy diet, and exercise, for the prevention and treatment of common chronic diseases and ailments.[12]

- *Reminiscence therapy:* The practice of reviewing past experiences to increase meaning was introduced in the 1960s by geriatric psychiatrist Robert Butler to help people find meaning at the end of life. It is now recognized as a powerful tool for psychological well-being and a healthy tool throughout the aging process.[13]

- *Meditation:* Present in all major religions and cultures since recorded history, meditation is the purposeful act of focusing your attention to experience relaxation, personal growth, or transcendence.

- *Mindfulness:* Mindfulness is the practice of giving your total attention to the moment at hand.

In addition to improving overall well-being, each of these approaches offers unique ways to counteract some of the less positive common side effects of caregiving. Combining them, as Positive Caregiving does, can help you value the caregiving experience. It can also offer an opportunity to build your resilience in all facets of your life—including, but not limited to, your role as caregiver. Elements of each of these practices are incorporated into the four pillars of Positive Caregiving: perspective, savoring, reminiscence, and growth. Let's take a look at each one.

Pillar 1: Perspective

Accepting and embracing your worldview while using positive psychology to create new lenses for seeing and experiencing the world as a caregiver.

Lenses—or personal viewpoints—influence how you see and experience the world; in other words, your *perspective*. They color your worldview, and thus affect your emotions. In the Positive Caregiving framework, we intentionally look at the world through the lenses of gratitude, empathy, forgiveness, love, and awe.

Your particular lenses were created and are reinforced through factors that include your individual life experiences, roles, genetics, and personality, as well as your culture and geography.

Every person has unique lenses. Thus, how you view the world and how you react to *the exact same event* may be quite different than someone else experiencing the same thing.

Here's an example: In 2015, Tim Urban wrote a post on his popular blog *Wait but Why* where he reflected on his life using the lens that his time on earth—like everyone's—is finite. He posted an image similar to this one—it was graph with 90 squares, each representing one year of life.

A 90-YEAR HUMAN LIFE

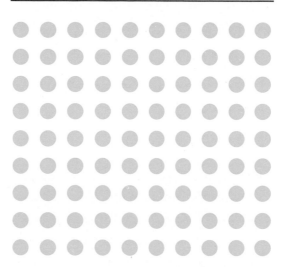

Then he calculated that, since he was 34 years old at the time, he would have 56 Super Bowls and 56 winters left if he lived to age 90. He wondered if knowing that number would change his experience of those events. Then Urban extrapolated how much time he could expect to spend with his older relatives: If he visited his parents—who were 60 years old at the time and lived in a different city—five times a year for a couple of days each time, he would have approximately 300 in-person days with them if they were all lucky enough to live another 30 years.

Right now, thinking of your own life this way, you may be experiencing positive or negative feelings. Another time you may feel differently. Why? Because different human beings approach, view, and react to the exact same information in very different ways at different times.

Nature, nurture, and your life experiences have given rise to your lenses, and thus your worldview. Yet your perspective *is* changeable. Some of this will happen naturally—as people age, they tend to get a bit more positive.[14] With a little intention and practice, you can also train your brain to adopt more optimistic lenses, and this is precisely what the Positive Caregiving exercises outlined in this book will help you do.

Most of the time we are not aware of our lenses, nor do we consciously interpret the world with our lenses in mind. But we know now that this can be altered with *intention* (also known as "reframing").

Through focused practice, you can train your brain to adopt a lens based on a particular positive emotion, even when living through a challenging life experience.

Specifically, the Positive Caregiving approach coaches you to reframe daily experiences through one of the following lenses:

 gratitude

 empathy

 forgiveness

 love

 awe

These lenses are not "prescriptions" for how to feel, or a way to avoid any negative feelings you may encounter. Rather, they help you *counteract the negative and provide a healthy path to resilience, balance, and coping.*[15] Employing the lenses that are built into each Positive Caregiving exercise is designed to help you access another pillar of the approach—savoring the moments of your life as they happen.

Pillar 2: Savoring

Using techniques from mindfulness and meditation to become more present and more aware of your experiences of positive emotions.

Robin's mom, Diana, was staying with Robin and her family as she was recuperating from cataract surgery. Robin had made up a bed on one of the couches on the first floor to make it easier for her mother to get around, and she seemed to be progressing well. Since Robin had taken a few days off work, she was thankful to be able to catch up on some chores. As she walked through the living room on her way to the laundry room, she glanced over to the couch where her mom was resting and stopped. Her 6-year-old son Darius had nestled up to her mom and their dog, Chester, was curled up at her feet. They were all asleep and looked so peaceful. Robin stood there for a few minutes, feeling a deep love and gratitude in the moment.

I'm sure you've heard sayings like "Stop and smell the roses" and "Enjoy the little things in life." But how often are you actually able to engage in this kind of awareness? If you're like most people, the answer to that question is not very often or not often enough.

Slowing down enough to pay attention to your experience in this very moment is so much more than a platitude. In fact, savoring, a concept coined by social psychologist Fred Bryant, Ph.D., is so important that hundreds of studies have found that it is highly connected to resilience and can be a powerful counterbalance to negative emotions.

In a world where there is no shortage of challenges, savoring just may be our best defense. Let's start increasing your capacity for savoring right now by assessing your current experience of it. Answer these two simple questions honestly:

- Are you frequently aware of experiencing positive emotions in your everyday life?
- How often do you make an effort to hold on to these fleeting moments?

If your answers indicate that you aren't engaged in much savoring—if any—you are certainly not alone. In the hustle and bustle of life, it is easy to lose touch with the things that bring you joy. All too often we let the good moments pass without celebrating them—or sometimes without realizing that they are even happening.

Some people are "natural savorers." They tend to notice and appreciate positive experiences as they happen. These individuals are the lucky ones, as most people need to practice savoring as they would any other new skill. In other words, most of us require subtle reminders and clear instructions on how to cultivate the oh-so-beneficial art of savoring, which is where Positive Caregiving comes in.

Positive Caregiving provides a practical approach to harnessing the power of savoring, with exercises you can do on your own, as well as ideas for shared activities you can do with your care partner. These simple activities can help you be more present in the moment and hold on to joy longer—which is all you need to do to become better at savoring.

Savoring starts with mindfulness: the practice of giving your total attention to the moment at hand. It is enhanced by taking notice of all your senses and surroundings in the "now." And you can prolong savoring by being grateful and amazed by your experiences, *even when there is sadness, fear, and despair happening in parallel to the moments that have your full attention.*

Being present and savoring the moment helps you access many powerful positive emotions, including those that the Positive Caregiving approach is designed to elicit: gratitude, empathy, forgiveness, love, and awe.

It's not hard or time-consuming to access these emotions. They are already happening for you to some extent, as they are an integral part of the human experience, whether you are paying attention to them or not. Why not savor them, when doing so can help you gain access to the positive emotions that build resilience and make life so much sweeter—both for you and your care partner?

After all, this is dedicated time that you get to spend with your loved one, and precious time they get to spend with you. And, as I mentioned in the introduction, this time will come to an end. Savoring helps you appreciate your caregiving experience now, and to be able to look back on it fondly and without regret once it has passed—something you can practice by embracing the third pillar of Positive Caregiving: reminiscence.

Pillar 3: Reminiscence

Reflecting and reviewing past experiences to help you and your care partner make meaning out of current circumstances and life in general.

Cami had come home from college for the summer. Since her return she had been visiting her grandmother in memory care every week. Her grandma, Ellen, was living with vascular dementia, which caused her to have trouble with her short-term memory, yet her long-term memory continued to be quite keen. Each visit, Cami would bring a stack of family photos that her mom had given her to upload onto the computer. Some of the photos had writing on the back, but for the ones that didn't she thought Ellen might be able to help fill in the information.

"Grandma, who is this in this picture, do you remember where this was?" Cami asked.

"Oh yes, well, that was Jimmy and Louie with Dad and my Uncle Carl. That was after they had finished baling hay and were sitting out back at the farm," Ellen replied. "And can you see that horse in the background? His name was King. That was my horse," she said with bright eyes and a big smile.

Cami jotted down notes on the back of the photos, astonished at the way her grandma could recall the details, but even more amazed at how her grandma's face lit up with joy talking about King.

The benefits of reminiscence as people age have been documented in multiple studies over the past five decades—even for those who are living with memory decline. These benefits include increased cognition and reduced symptoms of depression.[16]

The basic process of remembering life events, loved ones, and experiences that have made you—and your care partner—who you are is a powerful way to make sense of your life. It can be a source of great satisfaction and comfort. Reminiscing with your care partner can also help strengthen your bond. And it invites you to experience positive emotions as you relive past experiences with new perspective.

Reminiscence paves the way for life review, which is a similar but more in-depth mental process that allows people to not only make sense of their lives but also to resolve any conflicts that may bubble up. The reflection and resolution life review fosters have been shown to decrease stress and anxiety and improve life satisfaction as people age.[17]

The Positive Caregiving approach builds reminiscence into your caregiving relationship through the use of questions that are core to the shared activities and in day-to-day personal practices. Sharing, communicating, and listening—key components of reminiscing with your care partner—are fundamental to the Positive Caregiving process and set the foundation for the fourth pillar, growth.

Pillar 4: Growth

Combining the principles of positive psychology and lifestyle medicine into personal practices that foster your own personal development even (especially!) during the daily realities of being a caregiver.

Teresa's Aunt Joyce had just turned 85 and was living with multiple chronic diseases. Teresa had always helped her aunt out since she lived the closest to her of all the family. It started out just a few hours per week but slowly it had become much more time consuming. One day, after spending an hour on the phone with her aunt's supplemental insurance company, Teresa could feel the frustration and resentment building inside her. She closed her eyes as she was put on hold again. She breathed in with a deep long breath and let out a slow vocal sigh. When she opened her eyes, she spotted a squirrel burying black walnuts in the yard and was reminded what fun she had picking up walnuts in Joyce's yard with her siblings growing up. She thought about her Aunt Joyce and how she was always so patient with them—she never raised her voice even when they were being ornery. She felt the stress inside her start to clear. When the next claims agent answered, she kindly asked her questions again.

All humans have the ability to grow emotionally, socially, and spiritually throughout their lifetimes. While all of life's experiences can teach and shape us, giving and receiving care both provide ideal opportunities for personal growth. Although it can be frustrating, having your normal day-to-day routine disrupted and altered is also an occasion to let go of acting and thinking as you always have and develop new approaches, beliefs, and insights. It offers a chance to put life into perspective, to reflect, and to reassess what matters to you the most. Personal growth is a natural consequence of this reassessment.

Positive Caregiving makes growth an aim by providing instruction on how to reframe your experiences using the power of positive emotions and by offering guidance on how to strengthen your relationships with your loved ones. It also incorporates practices from lifestyle medicine that empower you to take care of your body, mind, and soul—even while caring for someone else. These "personal practices," offered as add-ons to shared activities that you can do with your care partner, encourage small behavioral changes in your daily habits to help strengthen and support your whole being. This mix of mindfulness techniques, ideas for getting more restorative sleep, and small nutritional changes can help build a stronger you from the inside out, even while supporting your care partner. These are changes that can last a lifetime and have a profound impact on health and well-being.

The first three pillars of Positive Caregiving—perspective, savoring, and reminiscence—all fuel your growth by helping you access the inner resources to change any behaviors that need to be changed for you to become stronger, healthier, and more resilient. The earlier you acknowledge caregiving as an opportunity for growth and frame it as a gift, the more quickly you will start to create lasting beneficial changes.

The Positive Emotions That Run Through Each of the Pillars

Science has shown that a person's well-being is directly correlated to their *ability to counteract negative emotions in a healthy way*. And strengthening your connection to positive emotions is a powerful way to do just that. That's why all the activities involved in the Positive Caregiving approach are designed to awaken one of the positive emotions of gratitude, empathy, forgiveness, love, and awe.

These five emotions offer a counterbalance to the negative emotions that are common and reoccurring throughout life, including during the caregiving experience. In the next five chapters, we'll look at each of these five positive emotions and their incredible power to change your outlook, health, and life for the better. I've also included exercises you can do that are geared toward helping you experience a specific positive emotion or are designed to infuse a certain daily task of caregiving with positive emotions, depending on your need and desire that day.

Each exercise includes:

- *Activity inspiration/reflection:* A quote from a well-regarded thinker that offers a thoughtful perspective on that positive emotion.

- *Shared activity:* Instructions for something you and your care partner can do together to invite that particular positive emotion.

- *"Let's talk"/reminisce:* Conversation starters that encourage the acts of reminiscing, listening, and sharing.

- *Caregiver personal practice:* A practical exercise that will help you support your own well-being and improve your mental, physical, and emotional wellness during your caregiving journey.

Combining Familiar Ingredients into a New Recipe

There is nothing new about the components of Positive Caregiving—they just have not yet been systematically combined and applied to the act of caregiving before. By clearly outlining the combination as I have done in this chapter, I'm aiming to help make the power of these tools more visible to you. It's much like the process of learning the name for something you have only ever felt intuitively before you can bring that thing into richer focus.

For example, have you ever been on a walk and been stopped by the sight of sunlight shining through the trees, being filtered by the leaves, and casting visible rays down to the earth? While there is no single word for this experience in English, in Japanese there is a word to capture this beauty: *komorebi*, pronounced koh-moh-reh-bee.

Even as a young child when I observed this in nature I was moved by the sight. It made me feel energized, and in awe. But it was not until I was in my late 40s that I learned of this term—*komorebi*—that put a name to my experience. The simple act of learning the term has changed my awareness and appreciation of the phenomenon, and it has enhanced my propensity to savor the moment. Now, rather than waiting to become aware of the sun filtering through the trees and leaves around me, I actively look for *komorebi* daily.

This shift has changed my life, and my perspective, immensely. And that is exactly what I hope outlining the pillars of Positive Caregiving will do for you, too—help draw your attention to these beautiful and powerful tools that have been there all along, but that perhaps you had not taken note of before.

Chapter 2 in Review

The four pillars of Positive Caregiving are based on a blend of positive psychology, lifestyle medicine, reminiscence therapy, meditation, and mindfulness.

Pillar 1: Perspective

Accepting and embracing your worldview while using positive psychology to create new lenses for seeing and experiencing the world as a caregiver.

Pillar 2: Savoring

Using techniques from mindfulness and meditation to become more present and more aware of your experiences of positive emotions.

Pillar 3: Reminiscence

Reflecting and reviewing past experiences to help you and your care partner make meaning out of current circumstances and life in general.

Pillar 4: Growth

Combining the principles of positive psychology and lifestyle medicine into personal practices that foster your own personal development even (especially!) during the daily realities of being a caregiver.

PART 2

The Positive Emotions That Will Enrich Your Experience

*"Gratitude bestows reverence,
allowing us to encounter
everyday epiphanies, those
transcendent moments of awe
that change forever how we
experience life and the world."*
—Sarah Ban Breathnach (1947–)

 *Chapter 3*

Gratitude

It had been a little more than four years since Amy's mom had been diagnosed with Alzheimer's disease. Since that time, Amy had moved closer to her mother and arranged for in-home care to supplement her own efforts to keep her mother in her home as long as possible. As her mother's dementia began increasingly to affect her communication, memory, and behavior, Amy was experiencing a variety of conflicting feelings. She felt frustration, even anger, at times when communication with her mother seemed impossible. She felt guilt, because she knew at some point in the near future she would need to find a memory care home for her mom. And she felt waves of sadness and grief as she contemplated this whole experience for both her mom and herself.

One morning, Amy and her mom were sitting in silence on the wooden deck of her mother's home. All of a sudden, Amy's mom turned to her and said, "Look at the sky. Isn't this just a beautiful morning? I am so thankful to be here with you." Amy was taken aback, not just because her mom hadn't been as communicative lately, but because of her mother's wisdom and strength that shined through in that moment despite the losses caused by her dementia. The experience left Amy both grateful and profoundly moved at the same time. She took a deep breath, squeezed her mom's hand, and tried to make the moment last as long as possible.

Amy would later recall how she replayed that moment over and over in her head when she was feeling depleted, stressed, or overwhelmed with sadness. She also made a special effort to look at the sky each morning and give thanks for the time with her mom. This gratitude helped her deal better with the challenges she encountered and reminded her to relish her role as a caregiver.

Gratitude—along with empathy, love, forgiveness, and awe—is core to the Positive Caregiving framework.

Gratitude is simply the feeling that comes when we appreciate something or someone in our lives. Some people are quick to give thanks for the world around them. Many people can easily recount things that they are grateful for, and most people can recall a moment or event where they felt a great sense of satisfaction, contentment, and gratefulness—like everything was right in the world. But gratitude can also be practiced, induced, and cultivated.[18] And this is good news, because gratitude has many powerful benefits.

In multiple studies, gratitude has been associated with increased feelings of well-being, resilience, generosity, and longevity.[19] People who feel or practice gratitude frequently report less stress and fewer occurrences of depression. They may even be rewiring their brains so that they come to focus more attentively on the positives.[20] In one study of residents living at a long-term care community, researchers found that the simple act of grateful reminiscence—when residents were asked to talk about what they were thankful for each evening at their shared dining tables—helped improve measures of overall well-being and hopefulness.[21] Similarly, simply writing down three good things in your life and reflecting on their causes—a hallmark exercise of positive psychology developed by its founder, Martin Seligman—each day for *only one week* was shown to increase happiness and decrease depressive symptoms for *up to six months.*[22]

How can something so simple have such profound—and long-lasting—effects? Feeling gratitude activates certain feel-good neurochemicals, which may explain some of its power. The brain releases dopamine, serotonin, and oxytocin when you are feeling grateful, and this may result in feelings of closeness, connection, and happiness. Physically, these neurochemicals help moderate the body's stress response system, and reducing the physiological effects of stress can produce increases in overall well-being.

Gratitude can be a gateway to additional positive emotions—a concept brought to the fore by Barbara L. Fredrickson, PhD., who theorized that positive emotions often "broaden and build" upon one another.[23] Feeling grateful can spur feelings of empathy, forgiveness, love, and awe, and this is the spiral that we are aiming for in the Positive Caregiving framework because it can lead to personal growth, increased connection to others, and improved life satisfaction.

Let's warm up by getting you (and your care partner) thinking about gratitude in your own lives. You can do this on your own first and then explore it with your care partner, or you may choose to do this together from the start. Either way will help get you into a grateful mindset and set the tone for thinking about Positive Caregiving and the core emotions that it aims to strengthen.

Exploring Gratitude in Your Own Lives

- How does experiencing gratitude *feel* to you? For example, do you feel a warmth inside, find yourself smiling, let out a happy sigh, or feel a sense of comfort? Take some time to really contemplate some of your own personal experiences with gratitude and discuss them with your care partner. Ask your care partner about some of their own experiences with gratitude. How are your experiences the same, and how are they different?

- What are some things that you often find yourself feeling grateful for—for example, family and friends or small acts of kindness? Again, take time to discuss these things with your care partner as an opportunity to learn more about each other.

- How often do you find yourself feeling grateful? Talk with your care partner about your answers.

There are no right or wrong answers to these questions. Just as factors such as your personality and life experience influence your perspective or worldview, these things also influence how you feel gratitude and other positive emotions. Practicing the activities included in this book will expand your baseline ability to feel gratitude, as well as the other positive emotions that tend to follow along on its heels.

Gratitude Practices

Now let's look at some shared activities that you can do as caregivers with your care partners to cultivate gratitude in your lives, while savoring the day together. (In Chapter 8, we will explore additional ways to incorporate gratitude into common, everyday activities.) Each shared activity starts with a quote for inspiration and features a list of conversation-starting questions for reminiscing with your care partner. Also accompanying each shared activity is a separate personal practice, an activity to support you in your role as a caregiver. You may want to use a dedicated journal to record your experiences or aid in activities. You may also download the Positive Caregiving mobile app, which lets you record your shared activities (reflections and photos) in an album for future reminiscence and review.

NEIGHBOR APPRECIATION

"A good neighbor is a priceless treasure."

—Chinese proverb

Building good relationships with neighbors helps create community trust. Neighbors can also be a source of support and comfort. Show one or more of your care partner's neighbors appreciation today, perhaps with a small bouquet of flowers, lemonade, or cookies. Or one of you could sweep their walk, leave a plant in front of their door, or give them a handwritten note of gratitude. Choose whatever you and your care partner would like to do and can do to show appreciation for the neighbors. If you don't know your care partner's neighbors or if there is someone new to the neighborhood you have yet to meet, reach out to them with at least an introduction, and perhaps a small gift.

- How well do you know your neighbors?
- What can you tell me about your current neighbors?
- What do you remember about a neighbor you had growing up?
- Have you had a favorite neighbor in your life? Who were they and where are they now?

Contact lists.

Your care partner's neighbors can be a great support system. They can help run errands, pick up items at the store, or check in on your care partner if you are away or live remotely. For your reference, create a simple contact list with names, phone numbers, and emails of your care partner's neighbors. Doing the same with your own neighbors will build your own personal support network.

AN UNEXPECTED THANK-YOU

ACTIVITY INSPIRATION/REFLECTION:

> *"The deepest principle in human nature is the craving to be appreciated."*
>
> —William James (1842–1910)

SHARED ACTIVITY:

With your care partner, discuss someone or a few people in your lives who you believe probably don't get much praise. Perhaps it is the mail carrier, a grocery clerk you see often, or a personal physician. Get out some thank-you notes, stationery, or blank sheets of paper, and write them a quick thank-you. They don't need to be too long or formal—just a small gesture can make someone's day. Mail the notes, deliver them in person, or leave them where the recipients can find them.

A few sample notes of appreciation:

Sample 1:

> Dear [enter name],
>
> I just wanted to drop you a quick note to let you know how much I appreciate you and all that you do for our community. You always find a way to make my day brighter. The world needs more people like you! Thank you.

Sample 2:

> Dear [enter name]
>
> I just wanted to say thank you for being you. Your kindness is a gift to the world. I appreciate you. Thanks for all that you do.

LET'S TALK/REMINISCE:

- Who are some of the helpful people in your life you see often but don't know well?
- Is there someone you regularly see who always just makes you *feel* better?
- Do you remember receiving a surprise thank-you in the past?

CAREGIVER PERSONAL PRACTICE

Gratitude for you.

Take time today to show yourself a little gratitude by writing a quick thank-you note to yourself. In it, praise the things you have been doing for yourself that show you care about *you* in addition to recognizing the things you do for your care partner and other loved ones. Put the note somewhere you can easily revisit it when you are feeling underappreciated, or just need a little pick-me-up.

CELEBRATE SOMEONE'S GOOD NEWS

ACTIVITY INSPIRATION/REFLECTION:

"The more one meditates upon good thoughts, the better will be their world and the world at large."

—Confucius (551–479 BCE)

SHARED ACTIVITY:

Think of something that has happened to you or to your care partner that would be considered good news. Or maybe you have heard some good news about someone one of you cares about. Perhaps someone you know got a clean bill of health from their doctor after cancer treatment or ran their first 5K. Maybe one of your family members just announced a pregnancy or a new job. Talk about what could be celebrated with your care partner, and then have a mini-celebration today. Pour a glass of bubbles (sparkling wine, juice, or water), make or buy a cake or cookies, and even put up party decorations, if you'd like. Then give a toast and eat your special treats. You also might choose to send a congratulatory note to the person whose good news it is. Whichever way you choose to celebrate, make sure to consider gratitude's role in this opportunity to recognize achievements, milestones, or contributions.

LET'S TALK/REMINISCE:

- What is the best news you have heard recently?

- How do you learn about good news in your social circles?

- How do you like to share good news with others?

- What was the best news you ever remember hearing?

Little wins.

You don't have to reach a major milestone or achievement to celebrate. Recognize "little wins" on a regular basis as well. Tonight, as you lie down to sleep, think about a little win you had today. Maybe you took the stairs instead of the elevator. Maybe you said no to something you didn't want to do. Maybe you found time to read. Whatever you did, say thank you and give yourself a pat on the back for a job well done.

EXPLORING AFFIRMATIONS

ACTIVITY INSPIRATION/REFLECTION:

"While I live, I hope."

—Nellie Bly (1864–1922)

SHARED ACTIVITY:

Affirmations are positive statements that describe a desired state or outcome—for example, "I choose to be patient." Whether written or spoken, these phrases can help change our thought patterns, improve our resilience, and mitigate stress. But here's the catch: affirmations need to be realistic and believable in order to reap their optimal benefits. Today, with your care partner, come up with one or two affirmations that speak to you as individuals and that you can recite to yourself three to five times per day. Next, see if you can challenge yourselves to incorporate your affirmation practice for a week, a month, or even a year.

Here are some sample affirmations to get you started:

- I choose to be calm.
- I am resilient in the face of challenges.
- Every obstacle is an opportunity to learn.
- I am strong in mind, body, and spirit.
- I am doing the best I can.

There are also a variety of mobile apps you can look to for daily positive affirmations, including ThinkUp, Shine, and Positive Caregiving's own app.

LET'S TALK/REMINISCE:

- Do you have a favorite affirmation?
- Who often gives you words of encouragement?
- What are some of the things you recite to yourself to give you strength or courage?
- Has there been a time in your life when you used positive affirmations to help you persevere?

CAREGIVER PERSONAL PRACTICE

Caregiver affirmations.

Affirmations can lower stress and curb negative rumination. Today's caregiver affirmation is, "I care deeply and unconditionally." Repeat it to yourself five times. As an added benefit, try reciting this affirmation in parallel to slow, deep breathing. Inhale ("I care deeply . . ."). Exhale (". . .and unconditionally"). Inhale ("I care deeply. . ."). Exhale (". . . and unconditionally").

REACHING OUT

ACTIVITY INSPIRATION/REFLECTION:

"I awoke this morning with devout thanksgiving for my friends, the old and new."

—Ralph Waldo Emerson (1803–1882)

SHARED ACTIVITY:

Today, each of you choose one person in your lives you haven't spoken to in a while and reach out to them. Whether you give them a call, send them a note or text, or shoot them an email, your goal is to let them know how grateful you are for them.

- Who did you reach out to? What is your favorite story about this person?

- Do you have any photos of you with this person that you can share?

- How did the two of you meet?

- What makes this person such an influential and important person in your life?

CAREGIVER PERSONAL PRACTICE

Social support system.

Social support is important at every stage in life, and it is especially important to nurture as we age. Our social circles can contribute to both mental and physical well-being, helping boost memory and longevity while decreasing stress and isolation. Use your activity time today to reach out and schedule some time with a friend, whether it's via a video call, on the phone, or in person. Also, if they're local, consider arranging to exercise with them—for instance, take a long walk together. That way you can experience the benefits of the feel-good chemicals that accompany movement at the same time as you experience the benefits of connection—just one more thing to be thankful for.

GRATEFUL LISTS

"Gratitude is not only the greatest of virtues, but the parent of all others."

—Cicero (106–43 BCE)

SHARED ACTIVITY:

Grab a couple sheets of paper and two writing tools, and sit down with your care partner. On the top of both papers, write: "I am grateful for . . ." Then, each of you list five things for which you are grateful. Afterward, read your lists to each other. You also may choose to decorate your sheets of paper with colors, markers, or paints. To remind yourselves of the many things for which you are grateful, consider hanging the finished products somewhere prominent, like on the refrigerator. Returning to a state of gratefulness on a regular basis can help rewire your brains to focus on the positives.

LET'S TALK/REMINISCE:

- What are you most grateful for at this moment?
- What is your favorite way to be shown gratitude?
- What are your favorite ways to show your gratitude to others?

CAREGIVER PERSONAL PRACTICE

Grateful state.

Today, as you are cleaning up after a meal, think of five things you are grateful for around and within your home. No need to write these things down; just make a mental list.

ROOM BY ROOM

ACTIVITY INSPIRATION/REFLECTION:

> *"Wear gratitude like a cloak and it will feed every corner of your life."*
>
> —Rumi (1207–1273)

SHARED ACTIVITY:

Together with your care partner, take a tour of the house. Stop in each room and look around. Room by room, point out what you love and value in your home. Maybe it's a picture, a bracelet, or a piece of hand-me-down furniture. Talk about the stories these things elicit. Take these moments to be thankful for your home and the things that surround you.

- What are some of your favorite items in each room?

- Is there anything that you would like to give more prominence or display differently?

- Are there any pieces of furniture or other items that bring up special memories or stories from the past?

CAREGIVER PERSONAL PRACTICE

Nightstand love.

A simple measure to help calm your mind and improve your sleep is to keep your bedside table functional and clear of clutter. Take a few minutes to organize the contents of your nightstand. Throw out or store items that aren't essential to a good night's sleep. Add a small tray to hold a glass of water. Have some tissues handy. Make sure charger cords are wound up and easily accessed. Keep a few books to peruse. Add a small wastebasket near the bed to help keep the table free of waste.

THE PERFECT MORNING

"And the sun laughed high in the infinite sky."

—Alice Dunbar Nelson (1875–1935)

SHARED ACTIVITY:

With your care partner, reflect on your ideas of a perfect morning. What does your perfect morning entail? A cup of coffee or tea? A beautiful sunrise or sleeping in? Quiet or music? Pancakes or pastries? Are there similarities in your ideas of a perfect morning? Is there something from each of your lists that you could incorporate into this morning's experience?

LET'S TALK/REMINISCE:

- What does a perfect morning look like to you?
- What is your favorite breakfast?
- If you could change one thing about your morning routine, what would it be?
- Are you an early bird or a late riser? Have you always been this way?

CAREGIVER PERSONAL PRACTICE

Lift up your morning.

Keeping some things that are special for you (and just for you) is important as a caregiver. Today think about the things that make your morning brighter. Maybe it is your morning coffee, a walk, or meditation. Have you lost some of these morning rituals in your role as a caregiver? Contemplate what you can do to get the start of your day back on track.

Chapter 3 in Review

- Gratitude is simply the feeling that comes when we appreciate something or someone in our lives.

- Gratitude has been shown to increase well-being, resilience, generosity, and longevity, and to reduce stress and depression. It also has the potential to rewire the brain to be more focused on positive rather than negative things.

- Gratitude elicits the release of feel-good neu-rochemicals including dopamine, serotonin, and oxytocin, which help foster feelings of closeness, connection, and happiness.

- Gratitude is a gateway to other positive emotions.

"To have compassion for those who suffer is a human quality which everyone should possess, especially those who have required comfort themselves in the past and have managed to find it in others."

—Giovanni Boccaccio (1313–1375)

 *Chapter 4*

Empathy

Bob and Susan had driven to the beach to get ice cream cones and to people-watch from the picnic shelter. Surprisingly, Susan told Bob that she wanted to take off her shoes and go to the shore to feel the waves cover her toes and slosh against her ankles. Bob, her husband of forty-eight years, didn't think that was a good idea. The sand was difficult to walk on and the waves could be unpredictable. He proclaimed it was too dangerous. What if she were to fall?

A woman sitting next to them on the grass over-heard their conversation. Amanda was a full-time nursing student, and she loved the water, too. She knew how it could refresh and rejuvenate as well as inspire, and she wasn't going to let Susan miss out on this therapy.

Amanda walked up to the couple and held out her hand. "I will take you down to the water, and don't worry, sir, I will help provide a steady hand for her to make it there safely," she said. Susan took off her sandals, while Amanda took hold of her arm and then supported her as they moved across the sand. As the waves came up farther onto the beach and touched the tips of their toes, Susan squealed with delight. As he listened to his wife enjoying herself, Bob realized this was therapy for him, too.

Empathy is our emotional ability to *feel* another's experience. Empathy can also be a cognitive experience, when you *think* about another person's experience in order to understand it in your own mind. When many people think about the concept of empathy, they tend to associate it with sharing in the negative emotional experiences of others, such as pain, sadness, or loss. But empathy is also being able to feel joy, pleasure, and satisfaction along with another person's experience.

Bob was able to tap into his emotional empathy when he realized how happy Susan was as she reached the water and could feel the waves roll over her toes. However, for caregivers, empathy isn't just about recognizing your care partner's feelings and needs; it is important in recognizing your own feelings and needs, too. When Bob's protective instincts had initially kicked in, his first reaction was to prohibit or at least argue against Susan walking to the water. By tapping into his own empathy for himself, he had a chance to acknowledge his own fears of her getting hurt, or if explored further, fears of losing Susan in general. These feelings, especially as you care for those you love, are natural, sometimes frightening, and may instinctively trigger your protective nature. But, as you lean into those emotions, and allow yourself to feel them, you can begin to temper them and balance them without hampering your care partner's own desires and wishes.

While some empathy can be accessed through cognition—as Bob's did—it is not required for emotional empathy. Dementia research has shown that even people living with cognitive disorders experience empathy and may even have heightened emotional responses to other people's emotions.

For instance, when they see someone who is irritated or frustrated, they may mirror those emotions without even knowing why.[24] Maintaining our ability to feel emotions as we age is critical to recognize in caregiving relationships, especially when caring for older adults—aging does not strip or diminish a person's yearning for joy. Indeed, remembering that the everyday pleasures that make life worth living are truly *ageless* and *essential* will help you have the empathy necessary to resolve any mixed feelings you may have and make the effort to provide these experiences for your care partner.

Empathy, or our ability to *feel* another's experience, as a concept dates back to the mid-19th century. Yet although empathy was defined only a few hundred years ago, we know that the human brain was hardwired for this emotion[25] and that our species has survived in part due to our ability to feel with and to respond to others with compassion. It is certainly key to caregiving at every phase of our lives.

Like gratitude, how people experience empathy depends on nature and nurture—or their genetics as well as their environment in early development.[26] Emotional empathy is innate for most humans and has been observed in infants as young as 10 months.[27] Cognitive empathy begins to develop in early childhood, around the ages of 3 to 4.[28] And, again, while cognitive empathy may decline with age, emotional empathy is believed to increase.[29]

Also, like gratitude (see Chapter 3), empathy is important for relationship satisfaction,[30] cooperation,[31] renewal, and replenishment.[32] Its presence also increases a person's compassionate or caring behavior.[33] Undoubtedly, empathy is vital to meaningful caregiving relationships.

Let's explore how you and your care partner experience empathy in your everyday lives.

Exploring Empathy in Your Own Lives

- How does experiencing empathy *feel* to you? Do you find yourself imagining or experiencing another's feelings easily? Are you quick to cry at emotional commercials or shows? Do you feel pangs inside when you see someone get physically hurt? Are you easily elated by someone's good fortune? With your care partner, discuss how you are the same and how are you different in how you experience empathy.

- How often do you find yourself feeling empathy for others around you? Talk about your answers.

- How has empathy influenced you and your care partner's own life decisions and choices? Discuss together.

Again, there are no right or wrong answers to these questions. Just as factors such as personality and life experiences influence how you feel gratitude (see Chapter 3), they also affect how you experience empathy. As you experiment with the empathy practices listed below, your answers may also evolve.

Empathy Practices

Here are some shared activities you can do with your care partner to cultivate empathy in both of your lives, as well as some activities you can do on your own. (In Chapter 8, we will explore additional ways to incorporate empathy into common, everyday activities.) Each shared activity starts with a quote for inspiration and features a list of conversation-starting questions for reminiscing with your care partner. Also accompanying each shared activity is a separate personal practice, an activity to support you in your role as a caregiver. You may want to use a dedicated journal to record your experiences or aid in activities. You may also download the Positive Caregiving mobile app, which lets you record your shared activities (reflections and photos) in an album for future reminiscence and review.

TRADING PLACES

*"There is no charm equal to
tenderness of the heart."*

—Jane Austen (1775–1817)

Empathy can help us increase our human connections and boost relationship satisfaction—something that is so important in the caregiving experience. Try putting yourselves in each other's shoes for a while to view life from the other's perspective. Take turns talking about your care partner relationship and what you imagine each other's current life experiences and perspectives to be. Discuss what surprises you the most about what the other says, and what changes you could make to your relationship based on your discussion.

- How would you describe each other's current daily experience?
- How closely aligned are your perceptions of your care partner's feelings with their own assessments?
- Is there anything surprising about how you or your care partner feels about the care partner experience?

- How might you change your behavior or communication with each other knowing what you know now?

Take a timeout.

In caregiving relationships, people sometimes say or do things they don't mean, and behind these actions are often feelings of fear, anxiety, or even physical pain. If this happens or something else starts aggravating you, choose to take a timeout— stop what you are doing, take a deep breath, and think about the big picture with empathy. Even step outside or out of the room momentarily. An occasional timeout can help alleviate daily stress.

CARE PARTNER MISSION STATEMENT

ACTIVITY INSPIRATION/REFLECTION:

"We must be true to each other."
—Lucy Stone (1818–1893)

SHARED ACTIVITY:

Organizations have long looked to mission statements to provide inspiration, direction, and alignment for customers, employees, and shareholders.

But have you ever thought about creating a mission statement for your personal relationships? Families who have created mission statements say they help provide a sense of comfort and clarity in times of life's inevitable challenges.

Craft a care partner mission statement with your care partner that encapsulates what makes your relationship special. Include what you wish for in the relationship and what you hope can help bring stability, comfort, and direction as you navigate caregiving. When you are done, post the statement on the refrigerator or anywhere you can easily see it, remember it, and reflect on it. This activity's conversation starters, listed below, can help you decide what you may want to include.

LET'S TALK/REMINISCE:

- What are your shared values?
- What would be the best outcomes from your care partner relationship?
- What is most important to you in this relationship—safety, love, hope, kindness, companionship, etc.?
- How would you describe a perfect care-partner relationship?

Here are a few sample care partner mission statements to inspire you:

Sample 1:

Our care partner mission is to create an environment of love and strive to savor every day together. We will honor and celebrate our unique abilities and adapt to the changes in our lives with grace.

Sample 2:

Our care partner mission is to be loving, forgiving, and patient. We will help each other become the best that we can be. We will try to laugh every day, be hopeful even amid fears, and let love and kindness guide our journey.

CAREGIVER PERSONAL PRACTICE

Personal mission statement.

The very process of writing a personal mission statement can help bring simplicity, direction, and hope to your life. To create your own personal mission statement, ask yourself some of the same questions that you used to create the care partner mission statement (above) or use those below to craft your own personal statement. Keep this mission statement in a place where you can always revisit it to remind yourself of your goals, hopes, and dreams.

- What are your most cherished values?
- What is most important to you in your relationships?
- What are your most important goals, hopes, and dreams?

MOON GAZING

"We are all one."

—Lakota prayer

Think of all humankind on earth and what things we share. For example, we all see the same moon. It is always there, orbiting our planet, pulling at the oceans. People often think of nighttime when they think of the moon, but the moon is often visible in the daytime, too. Today, go outside during the day to spot the moon. What can you see? What is its shape? Is it a full moon, or perhaps a crescent moon? The bluer the sky, the easier it will be to spot the moon. Then, as the sun goes down, go back outside to find the moon again. Think about all the other souls on earth who are viewing our moon at this very moment.

- Do you have a favorite type of moon?
- Do you remember the first moon landing?
- Do you have a favorite book or movie where the moon plays a special role?
- If you could travel to the moon, would you?

Half-moon moisturizing.

The small half-moon at the base of each fingernail is called a *lunula* (after the Latin word *luna*, meaning moon). Today, moisturize your cuticles around your nails with lotion or oil. Gently push the cuticles back to expose your *lunulaes*. There . . . don't your nails look better now, and didn't the process relax you just a bit? Good job taking care of yourself.

CARE BAG FOR SOMEONE IN NEED

ACTIVITY INSPIRATION/REFLECTION:

> *"We are all bound up together*
> *in one bundle of humanity..."*
>
> —Frances Ellen Watkins (1825–1911)

SHARED ACTIVITY:

Do you have toiletry samples stored in a bathroom drawer? Have you collected extra shampoo or soaps from hotel stays? Or perhaps you have kept toothpaste samples and toothbrushes from trips to your dentist. Gather some of these unused daily care items and put them into a bag.

Local city shelters, churches, and other community groups welcome these kinds of personal-care packages for those whom they serve, so drop one off next time you pass by the home of one of these organizations.

- How does helping others make you feel?
- What are some of the things that you use on a regular basis that would be hard to live without—even for a short while?
- Have you been the recipient of a helpful gift?
- What are some of your favorite memories of giving to others?

CAREGIVER PERSONAL PRACTICE

Stock up on staples.

Caregivers often have a long list of to-dos, and the workload can lead to overwhelming feelings and forgetfulness. Today, take inventory of the personal products that you use regularly—things like shampoo, floss, and soap. Are there things that you need to put on your list for the next store visit? Any extra items that you may want to have as a backup? Are there items that may be best subscribed to via a shopping delivery service? Little measures like this can help to keep you one step ahead, and it can be a relief to know there is one less thing to worry about.

MOSAIC MAGIC

"I am part of all that I have met."

—Alfred, Lord Tennyson (1809–1892)

SHARED ACTIVITY:

From ancient Romans to midcentury architectural artists, people across time have created mosaics using small pieces of glass, stone, or other colored materials held together with plaster to create larger pieces of art to decorate floors, walls, and even ceilings. You don't need to be Michelangelo to create your own mosaic, nor do you need to have plaster and stones sitting around the house. You and your care partner can create beautiful mosaics using paper and glue or even tape. You can tear magazines, colored papers, or even junk mail into pieces and arrange them onto another piece of paper, forming a design of your choice. Paint color samples can also be a great mosaic material—they provide a wide variety of colors and you can even choose your care partner's favorite colors as a starting point.

As you work on your creations, think about and discuss how your lives resemble a mosaic—how people, places, experiences, gains, and losses have come together to create your own lives. How have you become who you are based on all your experiences and relationships?

LET'S TALK/REMINISCE:

- Can you or your care partner recall where or when you saw a grand mosaic?

- Have you made a mosaic before?

- How has caregiving and care receiving become part of your life mosaic?

CAREGIVER PERSONAL PRACTICE

Others' masterpieces.

The concept of life mosaics can be a helpful mind-set when navigating the caregiver journey. Every health provider, service provider, and even your own care partner has their own life mosaic that makes them who they are. It can help to think about that simple fact with empathy to bolster your own patience and kindness when communication challenges, personality differences, or emotional reactions occur.

ATTEND A LOCAL PERFORMANCE

"Appreciation is a wonderful thing. It makes what is excellent in others belong to us as well."

—Voltaire (1694–1778)

SHARED ACTIVITY:

Attending live performances has been shown to help boost empathy. Today with your care partner, look at what shows, concerts, or other performances are being offered in your community this month. Check with your local high schools and colleges. Look up your local community calendar to see if there are any free performances happening soon that interest you. Whether it is a community play, a high school strings performance, or a free folk music concert in the park, make a plan for attending a local event with your care partner.

LET'S TALK/REMINISCE:

- Do you and/or your care partner attend performances in your community on a regular basis?

- Are there local groups that you enjoy watching the most?

- Have you ever performed in a live show?

- Is there a show or performance that you have always wanted to see live?

A round of applause.

Today, give yourself a round of applause or snaps for all that you do. Clap your hands or snap your fingers while taking time to consider how these actions feel. Take note of your hands and how they come together to make the clapping sound, or how your fingers work together to create a snap. On your final clap, or after your last snap, let your hands come together in a grasp. Hold them together for a moment while you take five deep breaths.

LIBRARY OR BOOKSTORE VISIT

ACTIVITY INSPIRATION/REFLECTION:

"That perfect tranquility of life which is nowhere to be found but in retreat, a faithful friend, and a good library."

—Aphra Behn (1640–1689)

Books provide a unique opportunity to connect with an author in a deeply cerebral way, and learning new things has many brain benefits. Do you visit the library routinely, or do you have a favorite bookstore that you go to on a regular basis? When was the last time you spent the afternoon perusing books? Together with your care partner choose a library or bookstore to visit today. Pick out a book for each other that is by an author you have not read or in a genre that you would normally skip. You may opt to choose a book of photos or illustrations (such as a travel, an art, or a coffee-table book) if your care partner finds reading difficult or no longer reads.

LET'S TALK/REMINISCE:

- What are your favorite sections of the library or bookstore?
- Do you prefer fiction or nonfiction? Why?
- What are some of your favorite books?

CAREGIVER PERSONAL PRACTICE

Getting in touch with the past.

Used books provide a wonderful opportunity to connect with others in another way. Used books have been held before. They have been read before.

Can you sense the hands that have held a used book that you have read and enjoyed? Imagine who these individual readers were, envision what they looked like, and think of what their life was like. Take a few deep breaths and offer your heart to the other readers who might have had a similar life-affirming, quiet exchange with the author.

SUPPORTING CAUSES

ACTIVITY INSPIRATION/REFLECTION:

"Use your voice for kindness, your ears for compassion, your hands for charity, your mind for truth, and your heart for love."

—Anonymous

SHARED ACTIVITY:

Talk with your care partner about organizations in your communities. Are there any that they have supported regularly with time or money? Have any causes become more important to them as they have aged? Together with your care partner, plan how you can support the causes that are important to you both—could you donate money, spread the word about their work to your circle, write to policy-makers, or volunteer at an upcoming event?

- What are the causes or nonprofits that mean the most to you?

- How did you first become involved or interested in your favorite causes?

- Do you currently volunteer or have you volunteered in your community?

- Is there a charity or nonprofit that you would like to be more involved with?

CAREGIVER PERSONAL PRACTICE

Immersive inspiration.

Use your hands to help immerse yourself physically into today's inspiration as you recite it quietly to yourself:

- "Use your voice for kindness." Place your fingertips on your throat.

- "Your ears for compassion." Move your hands over your ears.

- "Your hands for charity." Hold your hands in front of you.

- "Your mind for truth." Place your hands on the top of your head.

- "And your heart for love." Place your hands on your heart.

Repeat as many times as feels right for a calming, immersive meditation.

- Empathy is our emotional ability to *feel* another's experience.

- Empathy can also be a cognitive experience, when you *think* about another person's experience in order to understand it in your own mind.

- Through empathy, we can experience both the sadness and joys of others.

- Humans experience empathy throughout their lifespans—even into our latest years, and even if we experience cognitive impairment.

- Empathy contributes to relationship satisfaction, cooperation, renewal and replenishment, and compassionate behavior.

- Empathy is a critical underpinning of meaningful caregiving relationships.

"We pardon in the degree
that we love."
—François de La Rochefoucauld
(1613–1680)

 Chapter 5

Forgiveness

Claire's mom had spent

the past year in an assisted living community after experiencing a fall that required surgery and ongoing support. Her mom seemed to enjoy the residents and staff well enough, and she had made good progress in mobility with physical and occupational therapy, but she missed her family. She would call Claire often and ask her to visit.

Claire lived about 45 minutes away, the closest of four siblings to their mom's new home. She tried to make it to see her mom at least three times per week. With three kids of her own ages 13 to 17—all participating in multiple school activities—some weeks were more difficult than others.

It was a rainy Friday when Claire realized she might not get out to see her mom at all that week. A tremendous feeling of anxiety washed over her. Overwhelmed, she called her mom and told her that she wasn't going to make it, but that she would plan to visit on Monday. Despite the disappointment in her voice, Claire's mom told her not to worry about it. Addy, Claire's 14-year-old daughter, was riding in the car with Claire and overheard the conversation.

Addy said, "Mom, you do a lot for Grandma. She has friends and good care at her place. And you do so much for us. I am sure she will forgive you for not going to see her this week. You should forgive yourself."

Claire was taken back by Addy's insight, empathy, and wisdom. Like most people, Claire's go-to definition of forgiveness meant forgiving another person. But forgiving yourself is an important dimension of the overall concept of forgiveness, a core emotion in the Positive Caregiving framework. I define forgiveness simply as the act of letting go of negative feelings felt toward others or ourselves. Negative emotions or hurtful feelings, such as anger and frustration, impede our ability to experience positive emotions, like gratitude and love. Both forgiving others and forgiving yourself are vital in caregiving relationships and offer a variety of benefits. For caregivers, forgiveness can help you cope with challenges in your caregiving journey as well as reduce feelings of burden.[34]

There are varying degrees of forgiveness—from almost unimaginable forgiveness, such as when murder victims' families forgive their loved ones' killer, to more minor, mundane acts of forgiveness, like extending grace to a driver who cuts you off in traffic. As it relates to caregiving, there are also levels to forgiveness. There's self-forgiveness, as Claire's story highlights. There's also forgiveness of the things your care partner may do or say—or not do or say. Beyond that, your care partner may be someone who has hurt you in the past, where a deeper sense of forgiveness may be beneficial.

Forgiveness can feel like a tall order, but you don't just have to wait for it to happen on its own. Like gratitude and empathy, forgiveness can be practiced and nurtured on a regular basis.

Forgiveness has the power to improve emotional health[35] and life satisfaction—especially as we age.[36] It can also decrease psychological stress, anger, depression, and anxiety.[37] When we forgive, our bodies activate the limbic system, the system of nerves and networks in the brain that control basic emotions like happiness, anger, or fear.[38] This response has a calming effect and helps reduce our blood pressure, heart rate, and sweat response to stress.[39] It also helps our bodies by strengthening our immune system,[40] improving sleep quality,[41] and increasing our hope for the future.[42] The propensity to experience forgiveness may increase with age,[43] and may even promote longevity.[44] As more and more benefits of forgiveness have come to light recently, researchers and clinicians have begun to advocate for the use of forgiveness in clinical practice as a tool for improving the patient and caregiver experience.[45]

Let's explore how you and your care partner experience forgiveness in your everyday lives.

Exploring Forgiveness in Your Own Lives

- How does experiencing forgiveness *feel* to you? How does it feel to forgive others? How does it make you feel when you are forgiven? Ask your care partner these same questions and compare your answers.

- How often do you find yourself forgiving others around you? Talk about your answers.

- How often do you consciously forgive your-self? Discuss your answers.

- Has forgiveness changed you and your care partner's own lives? In what ways? Talk about your answers.

Again, there are no right or wrong answers to these questions. Just as factors such as personality and life experiences influence how you feel grati-tude (see Chapter 3) and empathy (see Chapter 4), they also affect how you experience forgiveness.

Forgiveness Practices

Here are activities you can do with your care part-ner—as well as some you can do on your own—to help you experience forgiveness in your lives, while savoring the day together. (In Chapter 8, we will explore additional ways to incorporate forgiveness into common, everyday activities.) Each shared activity starts with a quote for inspiration and fea-tures a list of conversation-starting questions for reminiscing with your care partner. Also accompa-nying each shared activity is a separate personal practice, an activity to support you in your role as a caregiver. You may want to use a dedicated journal to record your experiences or aid in activities. You may also download the Positive Caregiving mobile app, which lets you record your shared activities (reflections and photos) into an album for future reminiscence and review.

SAYING "I'M SORRY"

"The heart that is truly virtuous is ever inclined to pity and forgive the errors of its fellow-creatures."

—Susanna Rowson (1762–1824)

Simply saying "I'm sorry" to our loved ones when we have said something we didn't mean, or when we did something when we weren't thinking of all the consequences, can be a great release and a positive way to mend hearts. Each of you think about whether there was something said or done lately that you would like to say you're sorry for. Forgiving another has healing power for both you *and* that person. Talk with your care partner about your thoughts.

- Is there someone in your life you wish you could apologize to?
- Can you think of a time when you felt better by saying you were sorry?
- Is there something you would like to forgive yourself for?
- Do you say "I'm sorry" easily? Or do you tend to show your apologies through actions?

Self-apology.

Everyone deserves a little grace, and that is especially true for caregivers like you who are trying to juggle multiple responsibilities while being a rock for a care partner. Look in the mirror and say "I'm sorry" for anything you did today that you wish you hadn't. Then forgive yourself.

"DONE" LISTS

ACTIVITY INSPIRATION/REFLECTION:

"The beginning is always today."

—Mary Wollstonecraft (1759–1797)

SHARED ACTIVITY:

Together with your care partner, make a list of things that have been on your to-do list for far too long. They might be things like organize the garage, weed the flower bed, clean out the refrigerator, organize a drawer, or even something not chore-related, like making amends with someone. Making a list of what's on your mind is the first step. The second step is to choose one thing to do together today. Before you begin, tell each other that "we will let the rest go for today." Then release any irritation, anxiety, or stress that's holding you back. *Forgiving*, and then forgetting, paves the way to getting things done.

LET'S TALK/REMINISCE:

- What are your favorite chores to do?
- What are your least favorite chores?
- What were your chores when you were growing up?
- If you could snap your fingers and have one chore done, what would it be?

CAREGIVER PERSONAL PRACTICE

Ballooning.

As a caregiver, you will always have things on the to-do list. It is OK to *let go*. You are only one person, doing the best that you can, and the best that you can is a gift to your care partner. So forgive yourself for those things you haven't yet done in the following way: Imagine holding a helium balloon by a string. This balloon represents all the to-dos weighing you down. Imagine letting the string out of your hand and the balloon floating away.

LETTING GO OF REGRETS

*"How unhappy is he
who cannot forgive himself."*

—Publilius Syrus (85–43 BCE)

SHARED ACTIVITY:

Many people aim to live their lives with no regrets, but that isn't always how life goes. Inevitably there have been or will be choices, actions, and responses in our lives that we wish we could take back. Discuss with your care partner anything that you may feel remorse for, then vow aloud that you will do your best to move beyond any regrets.

LET'S TALK/REMINISCE:

- What are your biggest regrets?
- Are there things in you or your care partner's lives that you wish you could do over?
- What about things you regretted initially, but have come to see as a good thing over time?
- How can forgiveness aid in healing any regrets?

Ice cube meditation.

Today, perform an ice cube meditation. Place a small cube of ice in your hand and sit for a few minutes (or as long as is comfortable) watching it melt. Focus on its impermanence. Feel the cold solid slowly become liquid. Meditate on forgiveness all the while. When you are ready, toss the ice cube remains into the sink. Dry your hand and imagine forgiveness guiding you for the rest of the day.

AFTERNOON REST

ACTIVITY INSPIRATION/REFLECTION:

"Your legs will get heavy and tired. Then comes a moment of feeling the wings you've grown, lifting."

—Rumi (1207–1273)

SHARED ACTIVITY:

Researchers have identified several types of napping patterns that serve different functions for people. A "recovery" nap can help compensate for a bad night's sleep, while an "essential" nap may be necessary to help heal from an injury or illness. An "appetitive" nap, however, is done primarily for pleasure. A relaxing nap can help improve your mood and boost your energy, plus it provides a quiet time for introspection and a moment to practice forgiveness. Set aside 10 to 20 minutes for you and your care partner to simply lie down for a rest today—for a nap or for meditation or contemplation. Let forgiveness of another or forgiveness of yourself accompany you and when you awake or reappear from your rest, take notice if you feel lighter.

LET'S TALK/REMINISCE:

- Is a daily nap or afternoon rest part of your daily routine?
- Did you nap as a child?
- Where is your favorite spot to nap?

CAREGIVER PERSONAL PRACTICE

Getting in touch with your own energy.

Think about your own body, your own needs today. Get in tune with your recent energy levels. Are you running yourself down? Take time to give yourself forgiveness if you need to slow down.

ACCEPTING WHAT YOU CANNOT CHANGE

"None of us can know what we are capable of until we are tested."

—Elizabeth Blackwell (1826–1910)

SHARED ACTIVITY:

When life throws you curveballs, challenges your sense of "normal," or takes the wind right out of you, there can be a rush of negative feelings. Guilt, fear, and sadness can be overwhelming. Resilience in the face of adversity starts with accepting the things that we cannot change and forgiving ourselves for not being able to change things that are out of our control. Today with your care partner, discuss how current situations you cannot change can still be opportunities for personal or spiritual growth. Write these things down and place the lists in a safe place like a drawer or book. Schedule a day on your calendars to revisit the lists in a few months and then again in a year to see how life has unfolded.

LET'S TALK/REMINISCE:

- What good has come from your previous hardships?

- What have you learned about life by experiencing hardships in the past?
- Has forgiveness played a role in overcoming your hardships in the past? How?

Washing away stress.

Take a shower before bed. Imagine your worries and stresses being washed away. If you don't have time or energy for a shower, simply wash your face, taking time to wipe away gently any stress, resentment, or close-mindedness you may be holding.

FACE FEARS

ACTIVITY INSPIRATION/REFLECTION:

"You do not develop courage by being happy in your relationships every day. You develop it by surviving difficult times and challenging adversity."

—Epicurus (341–270 BCE)

We build courage and resilience by facing our fears. Being hopeful in the face of fear can help moderate some of the negative feelings such as stress and anxiety associated with fear. Sit down with your care partner and discuss each other's current fears. Have these feelings of fear been behind any negative actions, words, or behaviors lately that you would like to discuss? Use this time for forgiveness. Then take turns talking about how hope could help to counterbalance those fears.

LET'S TALK/REMINISCE:

- Is there something that is causing you to feel a great deal of fear now?
- What is the worst-case scenario?
- What is the likely outcome?
- What are some things that we can do to adapt and to be hopeful?

CAREGIVER PERSONAL PRACTICE

Friendly advice.

Think about any fears that may have percolated up today. In a moment of silence, close your eyes and think about what advice you would give to a friend experiencing what you are experiencing.

CREATIVE RELEASE

*"We are healed of a suffering only
by experiencing it to the full."*

—Marcel Proust (1871–1922)

SHARED ACTIVITY:

You don't need to be Picasso to express yourself through art. Creating art can be a brilliant
way to relieve stress. We know that creating art
also reduces anxiety, and may enhance cognitive
functioning and improve mobility. But have you
thought about how it can also help us to forgive?
Like creating art, forgiveness is a process. Get out
paints, pencils, crayons, or any type of art materials that you would like. Think about a difficult time
you have had. Draw it. Paint it. Color it. Express it
any way that you can. As you do, let go of what is
weighing you down. Picture forgiveness leaving
through your hands as you create.

LET'S TALK/REMINISCE:

- What is your favorite art medium?
- Is there a type of art that you have always
  wanted to try but haven't yet?
- How does creating art make you feel?
- What are your favorite colors and what feel-
  ings do they evoke?

Forgiveness focus.

Tonight before bed, give your hands some appreciation for the creative release and forgiveness experience that they provided you today as you made art. Coat your hands with lotion and place cotton gloves or socks over them while you sleep. When you awake, feel their renewed softness.

RECENT TENSIONS

ACTIVITY INSPIRATION/REFLECTION:

> *"May the bond of our true affection be knit ever more closely for all time."*
>
> **—Leoba (710–782)**

SHARED ACTIVITY:

Take a few moments to discuss with your care partner if there have been any recent tensions in your caregiving relationship. If none, celebrate! If there are, use some time today to discuss them, listening to each other's perspective. Sometimes talking it out is the best way to get through the tension and promote forgiveness.

- What are some of your pet peeves?

- If you could change one thing in your daily routine to help ease tension, what would it be?

- What are some of the things that just click or work well in your caregiving relationship?

- What are some things that always seem to help calm you down or relax when you feel tension?

CAREGIVER PERSONAL PRACTICE

Tension release.

For an instant tension release, clench your fists tightly for 30 seconds and then let go, opening your hands and stretching your fingers on an exhale. Feel the fear and stress leave through your fingertips. This simple technique has been shown to help relieve anxiety, and as a bonus may also help to boost memory and recall.

Chapter 5 in Review

- Forgiveness is letting go of negative feelings toward others or ourselves.

- There is a spectrum of forgiveness, from the dramatic to the mundane.

- Forgiving yourself is as important as forgiving other people.

- Forgiveness is a practice and a skill that can be nurtured over time—one that can improve emotional health and life satisfaction. Evidence even suggests that forgiveness helps you live longer.

- In regard to the caregiving relationship, forgiveness—of both yourself and your care partner—can lessen feelings of burden and help you find positive ways of coping with your role.

"Love is the bridge between
you and everything."

—Rumi (1207–1273)

 *Chapter 6*

Love

Maria poured a cup of coffee, added a few ounces of oat milk, and grabbed the bread out of the toaster. She spread a generous amount of apricot jam on each slice and took it into her father's room.

"I have to go to work, Dad," she said.

"Mmhmm," her dad replied.

"I will be home around 6. I will call you at noon to make sure you have taken your pills and to see how you are doing," she said as she leaned over and kissed the top of his head.

"I will pick up some food from Sun Garden on my way home. I will get you your regular!" she yelled as she ran out the door.

On her drive to work, Maria wondered if she was providing the best care that her dad needed. She just wanted him to be safe and happy, and hated leaving him alone all day. What she didn't realize was that even though she couldn't be with him at all times, knowing her father's preference for how he takes his coffee and toast, her attentiveness to his medication regimen, and her planning for a pleasurable meal at the end of the day were all mini-acts of love. She was filling his days with this positive emotion, even when she couldn't be physically present with him.

A caregiver's day is filled with hundreds of micro-moments of love that often don't even register in our own minds as such. I hope that by reading this book and engaging with the Positive Caregiving approach, you'll be able to identify all the micro-moments of love that your caregiving efforts elicit.

Over the past few decades, there have been many theories to define love, explore its purpose in human life, and understand how it is influenced by culture and biology.[46] According to research, one of the *universal* ways that humans feel love is when someone shows compassion toward them in difficult times.[47] Caregiving, therefore, is one of the most *loving* things we can do. If your feelings toward your care partner are complicated, focusing on feeling compassion for them can be an effective way to access the emotion of love within your relationship.

Some Benefits of Love

How does love affect your psychological and physical well-being? Let's first define what we mean by *love*. The ancient Greeks classified seven types of love, including *eros*, or romantic love; *storge*, or unconditional/familial love; and *agape*, the universal empathetic love.

The Greeks were onto something in their nuanced analysis of love, as people experience a wide range of loving emotions—of course there's a difference between loving pizza and the feeling of devotion and commitment you likely feel toward your care partner (along with other emotions).

Caregivers are often in attachment-love relationships with their care partners, for example, as spouses or as parent and child, and love is often a key motivator in caregiving.[48] This type of love is a real boon for caregivers, because when we feel it, our brains release the hormones oxytocin and vasopressin, which increase our desire to nurture the ones we love.[49]

Here within this book and in the model of Positive Caregiving, the activities I've included are designed specifically to elicit the experience of "felt love," which includes but is even broader than attachment-love.[50] Felt love includes all the types of love the Greeks defined, including those micro-moments in our life when we experience a flash of resonance with someone—someone we already know well, or even strangers.[51]

Before we dive into some of those activities, let's explore how you and your care partner experience love in your everyday lives.

Exploring Love in Your Own Lives

- How does experiencing love *feel* to you? Compare your answers with your care partner.

- Who are some of the people in your life whom you have deep attachment-love for? Talk about your answers.

- How do you express love to others? Discuss your answers.
- How do you show yourself self-love? Talk about your answers.

Again, there are no right or wrong answers to these questions. Just as factors such as personality and life experiences influence how you feel gratitude (see Chapter 3), empathy (see Chapter 4), and forgiveness (see Chapter 5), they also influence how you experience love.

Love Practices

Here are activities that you can do with your care partner or on your own to help invite feelings of love into your care partner experience. (In Chapter 8, we will explore additional ways to incorporate love into common, everyday activities.) Each shared activity starts with a quote for inspiration and features a list of conversation-starting questions for reminiscing with your care partner. Also accompanying each shared activity is a separate personal practice, an activity to support you in your role as a caregiver. You may want to use a dedicated journal to record your experiences or aid in activities. You may also download the Positive Caregiving mobile app, which lets you record your shared activities (reflections and photos) into an album for future reminiscence and review.

I LOVE YOU BECAUSE

*"I prize thy love more than
whole mines of gold."*

—Anne Bradstreet (1612–1672)

SHARED ACTIVITY:

Many days you might tell your care partner that you love them. Other days may pass when you don't say it at all. But it is likely rare that you sit down and tell each other what you really love about each other. Today, over a meal, talk about what you love about each other. If that's a little too intense, you can both take some time today to write each other a note with the specific things that you love about each other. Think about qualities and aspects both big and small, like your care partner's capacity for kindness. Your care partner might be grateful for the way you patiently help them climb the stairs. Whatever you truly appreciate about each other—share!

LET'S TALK/REMINISCE:

- What are your favorite qualities about each other?
- What do you love most about your care partner?
- What are some of the ways that you show love to each other?

CAREGIVER PERSONAL PRACTICE

Breathe in love, exhale fear.

Deep breathing is one of the quickest ways to decrease stress. By taking slow deep breaths, the body tells the brain to relax. A simple way to keep slow and steady breaths is to think "inhale love" as you inhale and "exhale fear" as you exhale. Repeat. Slow and steady.

MEMORY BOXES

ACTIVITY INSPIRATION/REFLECTION:

> *"A golden web of love is around us and beneath us."*
>
> **—Julia Ward Howe (1819–1910)**

SHARED ACTIVITY:

Memory boxes are simply containers to store a variety of mementos, photos, memorabilia, and items that remind us of special people, places, events, or time periods. Today with your care partner, look through meaningful items and sort them into memory boxes. Shoeboxes or other lidded containers work fine. Decorate the outside if you would like. You can use themes to organize them. For example, you might have a box for travel and one for holidays. Spend time identifying the feeling of love that these items evoke. Store the boxes somewhere that is easy to access for future reminiscence.

LET'S TALK/REMINISCE:

- Do you have a memory box?
- Where do you store your most cherished mementos?
- What items have you kept the longest to bring back specific memories?

CAREGIVER PERSONAL PRACTICE

Loved one's memory box.

Is there a loved one you are missing? Make a memory box to honor just them. Put some of the items that remind you the most of them in the box. You might add a few photos, special notes or cards, or a treasured book—anything that brings them back to you. Let the act of gathering these items call their love back to you.

RECORD A RELATIVE

*"What you leave behind is not
what is engraved in stone monuments,
but what is woven into the lives of others."*

—Pericles (495–429 BCE)

SHARED ACTIVITY:

Having family stories documented can be a gift to future generations. Film a video or voice-record a story that you would like to preserve for future generations. Some questions to get the masterpiece going are below.

LET'S TALK/REMINISCE:

- What was the most fun you have ever had?
- What are you the proudest of?
- What advice would you give future generations?
- What did you enjoy most about the way you were raised and your childhood?

CAREGIVER PERSONAL PRACTICE

Vocal cord soother.

Your voice is a gift to the world. Enjoy a vocal cord soother today by mixing warm water with a squeeze of lemon juice and honey to taste (roughly a teaspoon or so). Slowly sip and feel the elixir coat your throat as you swallow.

LOVE SONGS

"Every heart sings a song, incomplete, until another heart whispers back."

—Plato (427–347 BCE)

SHARED ACTIVITY:

Music, and especially music that arouses your emotions, is like magic in the brain. Even those who have damage to their brain's structure or a cognitive disorder that causes memory loss can remember tunes when they are played for them. This is likely due to the location in the brain where music memory is stored—the "music memory area" seems to be resistant to damage. Make a list of some of your favorite love songs and create a playlist today. There are many ways to create playlists for free. For example, you can create a playlist via Apple Music, Google Play Music, Amazon Music, or Spotify. Listen to your love song playlists during a meal or during an afternoon visit or card game.

- What songs come to mind when you think of love songs?
- What are your favorite love songs?
- What songs hold special meaning for you?
- Did you have a special love song played at your wedding or other special event?

CAREGIVER PERSONAL PRACTICE

Build your own "My Hug" playlist.

Music can reduce stress and even ease pain. Think of some of the songs you love or that make you feel good whenever you hear them. Then create a playlist just for yourself, name it "My Hug," and play it whenever you need a pick-me-up or to amplify joy.

FLOWER POWER

ACTIVITY INSPIRATION/REFLECTION:

"Let us choose for ourselves our path in life and let us try to strew that path with flowers."

—Émilie Du Châtelet (1706–1749)

People all over the world have been enjoying flowers for thousands of years. While flower types and colors may hold different meanings in different countries and cultures around the world, they are often given as a reminder of love. Make flowers part of your day today. Is your favorite flower in bloom, ready to be picked for a small bouquet? Or would today be a good day to plan for planting next year? Perhaps you would like to order some seeds for future use or visit a local flower shop.

- What is your favorite flower and why?
- Do you have special memories of these flowers?
- Are there special flowers that you always gift to a loved one on special days?

CAREGIVER PERSONAL PRACTICE

A bloom next to bed.

Show yourself a little extra love and bring some nature indoors by putting a bloom by your bed. Buy a flower, pick one from the garden, or even grab a stick of greens from a tree or shrub. Orchids can be an excellent choice for the bedroom, as they produce oxygen at night as well as during the day.

FAMILY TREES

"Families are like branches on a tree. We grow in different directions, yet our roots remain as one."

—Anonymous

SHARED ACTIVITY:

Even if you have studied your genealogy before, making actual family trees can be great for reminiscence and are fun to create. For this project you will need one or two pieces of paper and a couple of pencils or pens. How big of a tree do you want to create? Do you want to start with yourself? There are hundreds of free templates available online, but you can also simply start by writing your name in the center of the page and build your trees from there, starting with parents, any siblings, spouses, and children. Build out the tree and discuss your family members as well as what you love about each one of them as you go. As a bonus, consider adding photos to your tree.

LET'S TALK/REMINISCE:

- Have you studied your genealogy?
- Have you ever participated in genetic testing for ancestral data?
- How well do you know your ancestral roots?
- Do you and your care partner have your family trees documented?

Yoga tree pose.

In yoga, the tree pose helps strengthen the legs, feet, and core and provides a tool for grounding. Tonight, try the tree pose. Face a wall and put your hands on it for balance. Slowly move your weight to your right foot, keeping your right leg straight. Bend your left knee and bring your left foot flat to the inside of your right ankle, calf, or thigh (not your knee). Balance and hold as long as you are comfortable. Repeat on the other side.

Alternatively, if balance is a challenge, you can do reclining tree pose by lying down on your back and bringing one foot flat to the inside of the opposite straight leg. Reach your arms out to the side or overhead like branches. Hold the first side for several breaths. Repeat on the other side.

FRIENDS FOREVER

ACTIVITY INSPIRATION/REFLECTION:

"The balm of life, a kind and faithful friend."

—Mercy Otis Warren (1728–1814)

Some friendships last decades and some fade as our lives change. But, in each chapter of our lives, friends provide joy, comfort, companionship, and support. Think about your friendships. With your care partner, discuss the friends you have had the longest. What has kept that bond so tightly knit over the years? Then choose a friend from your past with whom you may have lost contact or with whom you don't often connect. Do you know where they are living now? Write them a note to say hi or to reminisce about a favorite memory.

LET'S TALK/REMINISCE:

- Who are your favorite childhood friends?
- What are some of your longest-lasting friendships?
- Who is the most recent friend you have made?

CAREGIVER PERSONAL PRACTICE

Hug it out.

Bring yourself to the here and now, and just *feel* better by giving a hug to someone. Embracing others releases oxytocin, a hormone that can help to relieve stress and pain, improve the immune system, and build stronger emotional bonds.

Chapter 6 in Review

- There are many different types of love. In this book, the focus is on felt love—those moments of resonance with and affection for another.

- The most universal experience of love is when we feel that someone else has compassion for us.

- Caregiving is one of the most loving acts you can do.

- If your feelings toward your care partner are complicated, focusing on feeling compassion for them can be an effective way to access the emotion of love within your relationship.

"The soul should always stand ajar, ready to welcome the ecstatic experience."

—Emily Dickinson (1830–1886)

 *Chapter 7*

Awe

Peter and Linda arrived at the long-awaited concert before many of the other attendees. Peter's Parkinson's disease often made him agitated in large crowds, but he insisted on going to the concert when it was announced that his favorite band would be coming to town.

The outdoor arena filled up and the band entered the stage. As the music started playing, Linda looked over at Peter and was warmed by his smile and trance-like gaze upon the band. After the concert on their drive home, Peter told Linda, "Sitting in the audience, listening to the band play all of their hits, it just made me feel so happy and at peace. I completely lost myself. I forgot about my Parkinson's for a bit. I feel so refreshed. Thank you for going with me." Linda was surprised by how uplifted Peter seemed. The next morning Peter continued to be in better spirits than he had been in a long time. Linda felt it was as if Peter's experience at the concert was some sort of reset for him. While she didn't fully understand why the experience had had such a powerful effect, she was thankful for it.

What Peter experienced at the concert was awe, a positive emotion of superpower proportions. Awe is that feeling where time seems to stop and you feel like you are connected to something bigger than yourself. The experience of awe can be described with words like amazement, elevation, fascination, and wonder.[52]

Until the early 2000s, awe had not been widely studied.[53] There has been an increased focus and a surge of research to learn more about this emotion since the turn of the millennium.[54]

Researchers have defined awe as "an emotional response to perceptually vast stimuli that transcends current frames of reference."[55] It has also been described as an "emotional connection to the inexplicable mystery of life,"[56] deemed the "peak aesthetic response,"[57] classified as a moderate self-transcendent experience,[58] and is most often associated with other positive emotions.[59]

Awe is often tied to experiences of nature, religion, music, and art. However, it also can be felt in many everyday environments and situations, and it can arrive in differing forms and sensations. For example, you may feel speechless, or make a vocal sound (similar to a slight gasp) reliably identified across cultures to communicate the emotion of awe.[60] In addition, facial displays are common, including a raising of the inner eyebrow, widening eyes, an opening and slightly dropping jaw, a slight jutting forward of the head, and visible inhaling.[61] Other physiological markers of awe may include chills or goosebumps, and in some cases tears.[62]

Regardless of how you experience awe, there are some powerful outcomes from its occurrence. For instance, experiencing awe can make you feel like you have more available time (that is, time seems to slow down as you immerse yourself in the moment),[63] increase your feelings of kindness and generosity,[64] help induce a positive mood,[65] spur your critical thinking, and give a boost to your immune system.[66]

While awe is often associated with being in the presence of natural wonders or man-made phenomenon, you don't need to be standing at the edge of the Grand Canyon or consumed in the middle of a concert to experience awe. It can occur even in the midst of daily life—looking up to notice a flock of geese passing overhead, observing a child sleeping or playing, or being reminded of our deep human connection to distant elders can all trigger a sense of awe. Let's explore how you and your care partner experience awe in your everyday lives.

Exploring Awe in Your Own Lives

- How does experiencing awe *feel* to you? Compare your answers with your care partner.

- What are the things that make you feel awe most often (for example, art, nature, music, human feats, etc.)? Talk about your answers.

- When was the last time you felt awe? Discuss your answers.

- Do you seek out feeling awe on a regular basis? Talk about your answers.

Again, there are no right or wrong answers to these questions. Awe is a profoundly subjective feeling. Just as factors such as your personality and life experiences influence the way you feel gratitude (see Chapter 3), empathy (see Chapter 4), forgiveness (see Chapter 5), and love (see Chapter 6), they also influence how you experience awe.

Awe Practices

Here are activities that you can do with your care partner—as well as some you can do on your own—that may help you to experience awe in your lives, while savoring the day together. (In Chapter 8, we will explore additional ways to incorporate awe into common, everyday activities.) Each shared activity starts with a quote for inspiration and features a list of conversation-starting questions for reminiscing with your care partner. Also accompanying each shared activity is a separate personal practice, an activity to support you in your role as a caregiver. You may want to use a dedicated journal to record your experiences or aid in activities. You may also download the Positive Caregiving mobile app, which lets you record your shared activities (reflections and photos) in an album for future reminiscence and review.

STARGAZING

"Silently, one by one, in the infinite meadows of heaven, blossomed the lovely stars, the forget-me-nots of the angels."

—Henry Wadsworth Longfellow (1807–1882)

SHARED ACTIVITY:

In the evening, if the weather allows, take a blanket or chairs outdoors. When you and your care partner are settled outside, look up. Take a few moments to breathe in the air and contemplate the grandness of the universe. To learn what you may see from your location this evening, search for NASA's Night Sky Planner online.

LET'S TALK/REMINISCE:

- Can you spot any planets or constellations?
- Have you ever seen a falling star?
- Did you have a telescope when you were growing up?
- Where have you viewed the best night skies?

Stardust within.

Stars are primarily made of hydrogen and helium, which are also the elements that cause them to shine brightly. Eventually, when a star runs out of this fuel, it may explode, sending its heavier elements, like carbon, iron, oxygen, and sulfur, into the atmosphere. Over millennia, these star remnants have fallen to Earth, where they are reused—even in the human body. This is why many scientists believe that we too are made of stars! Today your activity is to close your eyes and, with five deep breaths, get in tune with your body. Over the next few minutes, imagine the stardust within you. Feel your connection to the universe.

CLOUD WATCHING

ACTIVITY INSPIRATION/REFLECTION:

"Be comforted, dear soul! There is always light behind the clouds."

—Louisa May Alcott (1832–1888)

SHARED ACTIVITY:

Today with your care partner, sit outside or find a window for some awe-inspiring cloud watching. The four main types of clouds are *cumulus* (light, fluffy, cotton-like), *stratus* (large, low-lying), *cirrus* (thin, wispy), and *nimbus* (rain/snow). Clouds are an essential part of Earth's existence, as they help to regulate the planet's temperature and maintain its water supply. Clouds are good for our mental health as well: Cloud watching has been known to help with relaxation, focus, and imagination. So just sit back, relax, and let your imagination fly.

LET'S TALK/REMINISCE:

- When was the last time that you just watched the clouds go by?
- What shapes do you see?
- Can you identify what type of clouds you are viewing?
- Did you cloud watch when you were growing up?

CAREGIVER PERSONAL PRACTICE

Extraordinary individuality.

While there are four main different types of clouds, no two clouds are ever the same. Each one that you see is unique and fleeting, like a snowflake. As for humanity, every one of us is a unique individual unlike any other. Today, sit in quiet contemplation to reflect on the people who are closest to you. Think about their extraordinary individuality. And then consider the billions of people on earth who each represent a matchless being.

SACRED SPACES

"Places I love come back to me like music, hush me, and heal me when I am very tired."

—Sara Teasdale (1884–1933)

The word *sacred* means holy: something dedicated to a religious or spiritual purpose or deserving of veneration or reverence. Sacred spaces can help us transcend fear, give order to feelings of chaos, and provide a sense of deep belonging. Where are the nearby places, whether man-made or natural, that you and your care partner feel a reverence for— perhaps your places of worship, or maybe a spot in a nearby forest? Or it could be a location next to a body of water or a special tree. It may be a space within your home. Discuss spaces that are sacred to you and your care partner, and if you have the time and energy, visit one today.

- Where are the sacred spaces around you?
- What places or spaces make you just *feel* better?
- What places or spaces have or can evoke a feeling of awe for you?

- Was there a place or space you would go to when you were growing up that gave you a sense of comfort or awe?

Sacred in the mundane.

Looking for sacred places wherever we go, including in common spaces, is a practice that can help induce awe—and conversely experiencing awe and other positive emotions can make a place feel sacred. Today, practice getting in tune with wherever feels sacred to you where you would least expect it. For example, you might see a selfless act of kindness toward another at the grocery store or feel the warmth of sunshine on your arm while sitting in traffic.

ORDINARY WONDERS

ACTIVITY INSPIRATION/REFLECTION:

> *"The whole world is a series of miracles, but we're so used to them we call them ordinary things."*
>
> —Hans Christian Andersen (1805–1875)

Life can be fast and hectic, everything moving and swirling around. Most people don't take time to look around them and think about the ordinary wonders in our lives. Everything green around us started from a seed. All the trees, bushes, plants, weeds, and grass are programmed to grow. The foliage that surrounds us is incredibly diverse, whether we are in the city or country. The sun, the moon, the Earth: all are positioned perfectly to create the day and night, and the seasons. With your care partner, take notice of the season right now and talk about its highlights. There are hundreds of little wonders that we can slow down to contemplate. If you enjoy this activity and have the time, revisit it, focusing on every season that you experience where you live.

LET'S TALK/REMINISCE:

- What do you love about this season?
- What are your favorite memories from this season?
- How is the world right in front of you changing based on the season?
- Are there any things you would like to do before this season ends or that you are looking forward to next season?

Step outside.

Take a moment to step outside—no matter the weather. If the sun is out, savor the warmth of the sunshine on your skin. The natural light boosts serotonin in the brain, which then helps you feel more energetic, emotionally positive, and mentally focused. If there are clouds, take a deep breath and inhale the fresh air. Just being outdoors can help boost your mood, reduce stress, and help you feel more relaxed.

SEEDS

ACTIVITY INSPIRATION/REFLECTION:

"To see things in the seed, that is genius."

—Lao Tzu (c. 500 BCE)

SHARED ACTIVITY:

Planting seeds is a hopeful act. There is hope that the seeds we plant will provide us with a new bloom, a new food to consume, or simply something green. With your care partner, plant seeds in soil in a windowsill container of your choice. The slow and steady way that the plants unfold is an act of both patience and resilience and can be awe-inspiring. Keep the soil moist, but not too wet. Let the sun do the rest. When the seedlings are two to three inches tall, you may choose to replant them outside or just enjoy the new life in your home.

LET'S TALK/REMINISCE:

- Have you grown plants from seeds before?
- What are your favorite homegrown fruits or vegetables?
- Did you and your family grow plants from seeds when you were growing up? What kinds?

CAREGIVER PERSONAL PRACTICE

Hope planting.

Plant a seed of hope in your own mind. What is something you wish for? Is there something that seems like a long shot—a dream too big, or a task too difficult? Imagine yourself doing, becoming, accomplishing what you wish. Visualize your hope as a seed nestled deep in your center. Planted now, continue on with your day, knowing you have taken the first step in its becoming.

MEMORIES OF AWE

"To be thrilled by the stars at night; to be elated over a bird's nest or a wildflower in spring—these are some of the rewards of the simple life."

—John Burroughs (1837–1921)

SHARED ACTIVITY:

Being filled with awe does wonders for our mind and body. Talk with your care partner about your most memorable experiences of awe—that feeling where for a moment time stops and you feel like you are connected to something bigger than yourself. Perhaps you were somewhere in nature, or maybe at a concert. Possibly it was watching a leader speak or while standing in front of a magnificent architectural feat.

LET'S TALK/REMINISCE:

- Can you remember the first time you felt awe? Where were you?

- What have been some of your most memorable "awe" moments?

- Did any of these moments have a lasting effect on how you view the world?

- When was the last time you had a feeling of awe?

Merak.

Some words don't have comparable terms in English or other languages. For instance, *merak* (Serbian) is the word for a feeling of bliss and the sense of oneness with the universe that comes from the simplest of pleasures. In other words, the pursuit of small daily pleasures adds up to a great sense of happiness and fulfillment. *Merak:* what a wonderful word to contemplate today.

AMID THE TREES

ACTIVITY INSPIRATION/REFLECTION:

"I like trees because they seem more resigned to the way they have to live than other things do. I feel as if this tree knows everything I ever think of when I sit here. When I come back to it, I never have to remind it of anything; I just begin where I left off."

—Willa Cather (1873–1947)

Besides being the largest plants on Earth, trees play an essential role in the environment. As an air purifier, they remove carbon from our air and give us oxygen in return. They help to clean our soil and water and provide us shelter. Some trees have been alive for thousands of years, including the Methuselah Pine, found in the Inyo National Forest in California, which is believed to be close to 5,000 years old. Imagine if that tree could talk—the stories it could tell! Do you or your care partner have a favorite tree, or a tree that has a special meaning to you? Where is it located? Can you visit that tree today? If not, find a tree to sit under or walk around your neighborhood and admire the trees.

LET'S TALK/REMINISCE:

- What kind of trees do you like most?
- Is there a tree that holds a special meaning for you?
- What kind of trees did you have in your neighborhood or around your home when you were growing up?
- What are your favorite trees in spring? How about fall?

Komorebi.

Have you ever been on a walk and been moved by the sunlight shining through the trees, being filtered by the leaves, and casting rays down to the Earth? It can be an awe-inspiring sight. There is no single word for this phenomenon in English; however, in Japanese there is a word to capture this beauty: *komorebi* (pronounced koh-moh-reh-bee). In silence today, gently close your eyes and visualize yourself standing amid a grove of trees, sunlight shining down through the leaves. Imagine the warmth and the beauty. Think *komorebi, komorebi, komorebi* to yourself as you breathe deeply.

LOVE WITHOUT END

ACTIVITY INSPIRATION/REFLECTION:

> *"I have so much of you in my heart . . ."*
> —John Keats (1795–1821)

SHARED ACTIVITY:

The people we love, even in death, are never really gone. You can summon memories whenever you need comfort, which can be an awe-inducing experience. So much of who we are is influenced by the ones who we love, and that influence does not cease when they are no longer physically nearby. Today with your care partner, reminisce about some of the people in your life who are no longer here.

For each person you discuss:

- What was your relationship to this person?
- What special qualities about them do you miss the most?
- What lessons did they teach you?
- What message or advice do you think that they would give to you now, at this very moment?

CAREGIVER PERSONAL PRACTICE

Conversation across generations.

Today, find a quiet spot to contemplate your great-great-great-great grandparents and the other family members who are part of your lineage but whom you never met. Next, contemplate your great-great-great-great grandchildren or your descendants five generations from now who will never know you. Practice sitting with the love that is unnamed and unknown but passed from generation to generation. This contemplation of time can be awe-inducing.

Chapter 7 in Review

- Hallmarks of awe are feeling like time has slowed or stopped altogether and that you are connected to something bigger than yourself.

- Awe can be felt in the presence of nature, religion, or the arts, but it can also be accessed in the midst of daily life.

- Awe has been shown to increase feelings of kindness and generosity, bring on a more positive mood, inspire fresh thinking, and even give your immune system a boost.

PART 3

Applying Positive Caregiving to Your Daily Life

"The universe is full of magical things patiently waiting for our wits to grow sharper."

—Eden Phillpotts (1862–1960)

Chapter 8

Everyday Activities

It seems that the world is awash with messages and advice for people to be more grateful, empathetic, forgiving, loving, and awe-struck. You can't scroll through social media without seeing a meme or quote about gratitude or love. Yet, what I hear over and over from people is, "Yes, I know that gratitude or [insert another positive emotion here] is good for me, and it sounds nice, but *how?*"

Although it may seem complicated, the good news is that incorporating gratitude, empathy, forgiveness, love, and awe into your daily routine is simple once you get the hang of it. While the activities I've included so far in this book are useful tools, you don't even have to carve out special time to experience positive emotions—you can experience them as you go about your normal routines.

Walking, eating, driving, waiting—these parts of daily life provide the perfect opportunity to practice gratitude, empathy, forgiveness, love, and awe. When you infuse your everyday activities with positivity, you experience the good feelings they provide in the moment. Over time, you also raise your baseline propensity to seek out the positive.

In this chapter, I've included many simple ideas for bringing each of the five positive emotions in Positive Caregiving into your daily life. You may choose to give many of them a try, or you may find one or two that really speak to you or move the needle on your personal positivity meter. It's not the number of different activities you try that counts—it's remembering to do them when life is busy and hectic.

Whichever way you chose to approach or engage with these activity ideas, my hope is that with practice, you find yourself opening more easily and more often to the gifts of gratitude, empathy, forgiveness, love, and awe.

Walking

On occasion, physical challenges can prohibit long walks, walking without aid, or even walking at all. But for most people, walking is something you do every day. It's how you get around the house. It's also a main form of transportation outside the house, whether to the garden, the grocery, or the coffee shop. And walking is therapeutic, as it can lower blood pressure and improve mood and balance, as well as calm the nerves and clear the mind.

You may walk every day as a form of exercise, or you might just take an occasional stroll, or maybe you just want to start taking a few more steps every day. Regardless, the walking activities included will help you and your care partner infuse the experience with gratitude, empathy, forgiveness, love, and awe.

 GRATITUDE WALK

> *"An early morning walk is a blessing for the whole day."*
>
> —Henry David Thoreau (1817–1862)

SHARED ACTIVITY:

As you walk with your care partner today, make it a point to identify five things for which you are grateful. If you're outside, examples might include the trees, the fresh air, a bird flying overhead, sunshine, and a seasonal bloom. Consider recording your findings with your phone or in a notebook, or simply talk about them.

LET'S TALK/REMINISCE:

- Where are your favorite places to walk?
- If you could go for a walk anywhere in the world, where would it be?
- If you could go on a walk with anyone, past or present, who would it be?

CAREGIVER PERSONAL PRACTICE

Focus every step of the way.

Among its many benefits, walking also provides an opportunity for meditation. As you walk today, take time to focus on the steps. Feel the ground beneath your feet. Try thinking "thank you" as you step heel (thank) to toe (you) as a form of meditation.

 **EYE TO EYE**

ACTIVITY INSPIRATION/REFLECTION:

> *"The soul, fortunately, has an interpreter—often an unconscious but still a faithful interpreter—in the eye."*
>
> **—Charlotte Brontë (1816–1855)**

SHARED ACTIVITY:

On a walk with your care partner, greet each person you see with a smile, a hello, and/or a wave. Take time to recognize their humanity, their presence, their lives. Feel the connection you make with them and the empathy you feel. You may also walk to your favorite park bench, bus stop, or picnic table and greet others as they walk by.

- Do you enjoy talking with strangers?
- Is it easy for you to meet and connect with new people?
- Where do you find yourself people-watching?

CAREGIVER PERSONAL PRACTICE

Quiet connection.

Even if you aren't seeing your care partner today, make it a point as you walk through your daily life to meet people's (yes, even—especially—strangers') gazes to recharge your energy and give you a chance to experience empathy.

 # LABYRINTH WALK

ACTIVITY INSPIRATION/REFLECTION:

> *"One step at a time is all it takes to get you there."*
>
> —Emily Dickinson (1830–1886)

SHARED ACTIVITY:

Walk a labyrinth or a circular path with your care partner as an exercise of forgiveness. Use each step you take toward the center or around the path as an opportunity to reflect and bring you closer and closer to forgiveness, for yourself or others. You may choose to talk with your care partner about what you are working to forgive, or you may do this in your own quiet reflection. For help finding a labyrinth in your community, search online for "labyrinth locator."

- Have you become more forgiving as you have aged?

- Who is the most forgiving person you have ever known?

- Do you remember your first memory of forgiveness?

CAREGIVER PERSONAL PRACTICE

Focus on the journey.

Walks, whether in a labyrinth, a rounded path, or a stroll around the block, have a definitive start and stopping point. Try to imagine your path from above, following your movement as you begin, all the way to the end. Notice the journey, your incremental movement forward with each step, and acknowledge the power of your being able to move through time and space.

 **HEART WALK**

"A loving heart is the truest wisdom."

—Charles Dickens (1812–1870)

SHARED ACTIVITY:

The heart shape has become a universal symbol of love. On a walk with your care partner, be on the lookout for heart-shaped items. Leaves, rocks and stones, tree bark, signage, decorations—you might find a surprising number of heart-like shapes when you take time to look. Let them serve as visual reminders of love.

LET'S TALK/REMINISCE:

- Were you surprised at how many heart shapes you found?

- What other things besides hearts remind you of love?

- What is the most loving thing that has been done for you this week?

Heart love.

From watching our salt intake to increasing our vegetable consumption, there are many ways to take care of our own hearts at each meal. Some of the best foods for heart health include nuts, leafy greens, berries, and beans. Think about how you can add one or two heart-healthy foods to your meals this week.

 ## WIND WATCHING

ACTIVITY INSPIRATION/REFLECTION:

"My soul is awakened, my spirit is soaring, and carried aloft on the wings of the breeze."

—Anne Brontë (1820–1849)

SHARED ACTIVITY:

We know that the wind is there because we can feel it on our skin and in our hair. We can hear the wind blowing through trees, and we can see its effects in many ways: plants dancing, water rippling, and clouds rolling by. While you walk with your care partner, watch the wind and how it influences nature and humanity. Talk about all the ways you can "see" the wind. What ways are the most moving or amazing to you and to your care partner? Which are the most poetic? Are there any ways of "seeing" or feeling the wind that you have never thought of before?

LET'S TALK/REMINISCE:

- When has the wind charmed you, and when has it threatened?
- Has pleasure or fear caused by the wind brought you closer to others who shared the experience?
- Did you grow up in a place where wind was common?

CAREGIVER PERSONAL PRACTICE

One with the wind.

Breathing helps us be one with the wind: as we inhale, wind enters us; as we exhale, our breath leaves to rejoin the wind. Listen to your own breaths. Inhale through your nose and breathe out audibly through your mouth, maybe while vocalizing a "Hmmm" or an "Ohhh." Repeat as many times as you wish.

Eating is core to our human existence. Foods provide us with vitamins, nutrients, and fuel for our bodies. The pleasure that can come from a shared meal or a nostalgic menu feeds our souls as well. Many cherished memories may be entwined with holiday meals, or meals shared with loved ones on special occasions. For many people, meals are highlights of the day. Because most people eat at least a few times per day, this everyday activity gives us ample time to practice gratitude, empathy, forgiveness, love, and awe.

 # A TOAST!

ACTIVITY INSPIRATION/REFLECTION:

> *"For each new morning with its light,*
> *For rest and shelter of the night,*
> *For health and food, for love and friends,*
> *For everything Thy goodness sends."*
>
> —Ralph Waldo Emerson (1803–1882)

SHARED ACTIVITY:

Toasting, or offering a spoken gesture of gratitude, appreciation, or good will is an ancient and international tradition. Sometimes speckled with humor, sometimes purely heartfelt, offering a toast before, during, or after a meal is a simple way to practice gratitude with your care partner.

Write a toast to be given at dinner with a glass of sparkling wine, juice, or water, and ask your care partner to do the same. Whether it's a sentence or two, or a longer expression of gratitude, this shared offering and the clinking of glasses will make the meal extra special.

LET'S TALK/REMINISCE:

- Do you have a favorite toast?
- Have you ever given a toast to a large group or at an important event?
- Was toasting part of your family meals or holidays growing up?

CAREGIVER PERSONAL PRACTICE

A *caregiver's* toast.

Raise a toast to yourself today or any day. Raise your cup, mug, or glass and make up your own toast or quietly recite to yourself:

Here's to me and this one life I am living.

May my heart always lead the way.

✱ EXPLORING OUR WORLD THROUGH FOOD

"There are no strangers here, only friends you haven't yet met."

—**William Butler Yeats (1865–1939)**

SHARED ACTIVITY:

Foods are a reflection of our cultures and are gateways to our deepest sense of self, providing us with memories and great comfort. The very same ingredients are used in a wide variety of cuisines across the world, which reminds us of our similarities and diversity. Make or order a dish (or a meal) inspired by another country or culture that you and your care partner have never tried, then share it together. Learn about the food's heritage, history, and meaning in the culture it comes from.

LET'S TALK/REMINISCE:

- What foods are core to your own culture?
- What are some of the common dishes that represent your heritage that you love the most?
- Is there a kind of food that you have always wanted to try?
- Who are some of the people in your lives who have introduced different cuisines to you?

Hara hachi bu.

Based on Confucian wisdom, mindful eating follows the rule of *hara hachi bu*, which means to stop eating when 80 percent full. Try thinking *hara hachi bu* before your meals today and see how this mindfulness trick can keep your mind focused on your food, your belly satisfied, and your body happy.

 # CANDLELIGHT DINNER

ACTIVITY INSPIRATION/REFLECTION:

"Holding on to anger is like grasping a hot coal with the intent of throwing it at someone else; you are the one who gets burned."

—Buddha (563–483 BCE)

SHARED ACTIVITY:

Use a candlelight dinner as the path to forgiveness. Play soft music in the background and eat a favorite meal with your care partner by the light of candles. With each bite, imagine releasing what you wish to forgive, of yourself or others.

You can talk about your forgiveness intention with your care partner, or simply practice this act of forgiveness on your own. At the end of the meal, blow out the candles as a forgiveness meditation. Imagine letting go of any wrongs you have felt lately with the disappearance of the flame.

LET'S TALK/REMINISCE:

- Do you enjoy candlelight?
- Did your family light candles for special occasions growing up?
- What else besides candlelight can make a meal extra special?

CAREGIVER PERSONAL PRACTICE

Centering.

A simple visual cue, like the flame of a candle, can help you focus and center yourself. Light a candle, take a comfortable seat in direct sight of the candle, and rest your eyes on the flame. Try to stay in the present as you focus on the flickering light and take deep calming breaths for a few minutes before blowing out the flame.

💗 BAKE A FAMILY FAVORITE

"The secret ingredient to baking is love."

—Anonymous

SHARED ACTIVITY:

Baking a family favorite can bring back memories and fill your home and your hearts with love. Today pick a favorite family recipe for you and your care partner to bake together. Don't rush or be distracted: Take time to enjoy the process. Savor the love you put into it as you sample the final product.

LET'S TALK/REMINISCE:

- What are some of your family's favorite baked goods?
- Is there a baked good that is extra special to you?
- Is there a baked item that reminds you especially of your childhood?

Baking with presence.

Any kind of cooking can be a meditation, but baking gives us an opportunity to be 100 percent present with the recipes, which need to be more exact than in other forms of cooking. Embracing and focusing on being precise as you measure out ingredients transforms baking into a more mindful activity. Today, give yourself the gift of presence: presence with your care partner, and presence in the act of baking.

 **FOOD LINKS**

ACTIVITY INSPIRATION/REFLECTION:

"Realize that everything connects to everything else."

—Leonardo da Vinci (1452–1519)

SHARED ACTIVITY:

With your care partner, choose a meal to discuss the food sources and processes that made your meal happen. For instance, if you're enjoying a slice of pizza, consider the long cycle necessary for the creation of pizza. Wheat is grown, harvested, and ground into flour. Yeast is cultivated, grown, and dried, then processed for distribution. The sauce's tomatoes are grown in the sun, and the mozzarella is created from cow, buffalo, or even almond milk. And then, what about those favorite toppings on the pizza? Think about how sunlight and rain are essential to grow vegetables. We often don't take the time to think about how our meals come to be, yet this can provide for a fascinating conversation that can leave us in awe of the bounty of this earth.

LET'S TALK/REMINISCE:

- What are your favorite foods that are grown in the ground?
- What are your favorite foods that grow on trees?
- Did you have a garden growing up? If so, what did your family grow?

CAREGIVER PERSONAL PRACTICE

Luscious local foods.

Produce often starts to lose some of its nutritional values within 24 hours of being harvested. Local foods, or foods grown nearby, are more nutritious simply because the time that it takes from picking or harvesting to your own table is shorter. This week, make an effort to source a locally grown item or ingredient in a meal or for a snack. (Farmers' markets are great sources of local food, and make for a fun outing, too.)

Everyone has them. Someone must do them. Household chores are a part of most adults' day-to-day experience. From washing and folding clothes to doing the dishes, these common household tasks are often overlooked as opportunities to savor the day and to cherish quality time with our care partners.

Below you will find easy ideas to help incorporate gratitude, empathy, forgiveness, love, and awe into your daily life while getting some things checked off your to-do lists.

 **WINDOW WASHING**

ACTIVITY INSPIRATION/REFLECTION:

"If the doors of perception were cleansed, every thing would appear to man as it is, infinite."

—William Blake (1757–1827)

SHARED ACTIVITY:

Take a leisurely walk around the house with your care partner and look out the windows in each room. Consider cleaning some of the windows from the inside to make the view clearer and more refreshing. As you are cleaning the windows with your care partner, take some time to discuss today's inspiration from William Blake. How have you and your care partner's perceptions of life changed over the years? Have your perceptions changed lately?

LET'S TALK/REMINISCE:

- What are your favorite views or things to look at from each window?

- Did you notice some things outside that you have never noticed before?

- Is there a window that you look out more than others?

CAREGIVER PERSONAL PRACTICE

Clear-eyed.

It is common for caregivers to overlook their own personal needs. For example, when was the last time you had an eye exam? Simple vision screenings can help ensure you have the proper visual aids such as glasses or contacts to ease eye-strain as your eyes change. Comprehensive eye exams, on the other hand, are key components of health that help monitor your eyes for other age-related changes such as cataracts. Schedule an eye exam today if you haven't had one recently, so you can continue to notice the awesome things around you with ease.

 PANTRY CARE

"Be compassionate. Not just to your friends, but to everyone."

—The Bhagavad Gita (c. 200 BCE)

SHARED ACTIVITY:

Clean and organize the pantry or cupboard where you store canned and dry foods with your care partner. Rearrange them in easy-to-find rows or sections. While you are organizing, pick a few items to donate to the local food pantry. Deliver or drop off the goods with your care partner as an act of love and empathy for your fellow community members.

LET'S TALK/REMINISCE:

- What are your favorite pantry foods?
- Did your family can foods when you were growing up?
- Is there a special food bank or charity that you like to gift food or other household items to in your community?

MEMENTOS AS A GIFT OF FORGIVENESS

ACTIVITY INSPIRATION/REFLECTION

"When the heart weeps for what it has lost, the soul rejoices for what it has found."

—Sufi proverb

SHARED ACTIVITY:

Mementos are objects or items that serve to remind us of a person, place, or event. Cleaning and organizing your care partner's mementos while listening to the stories behind them is a wonderful way to engage in life review, and also an opportunity to identify and establish your care partner's wishes. Select a box, drawer, or shelf and explore your care partner's items together. Have your care partner identify items they think will also mean something to loved ones and write down their wishes in an informal list—this gesture is a gift that can help prevent dissension and family squabbles in the future. Giving a cherished item can also serve as an act of forgiveness. Ask your care partner if they would like to offer any item as a gesture of reconciliation or compassion to a family member or friend now.

LET'S TALK/REMINISCE:

- What are some meaningful gifts that were handed down to you from those you love?

- What are some of the mementos you have that mean the most to you?

- Has anyone given you a gift or memento as an offering of forgiveness?

CAREGIVER PERSONAL PRACTICE

Memento mori.

The word memento comes from the Latin phrase memento mori, which means *remember you must die.* Western cultures tend to be notoriously death-averse, yet thinking about our own mortality and humanity can be both motivating and life-affirming. It can help us to be more present and remind us to savor each and every day. Try contemplating memento mori as a tool to help put stressors and life in general in perspective.

💎 HOME ADAPTATIONS

> *"Life belongs to the living, and they who live must be prepared for the changes."*
>
> —Johann Wolfgang von Goethe (1749–1832)

In survey after survey, people indicate that they would prefer to stay in their own home as they age—and the majority Americans *do* age in place. While age-related changes can affect balance, sight, and dexterity, making home adaptations to ensure safety can be both an act of self-love for the care recipient and a gift of love to give to your care partner. There are many easy-to-do adaptations to help prevent falls, improve mobility, and just make life easier. Some of the adaptations that you and your care partner can put in place together include:

- Remove throw rugs (or tack them down).

- Wind up all cords and tie them in a way that keeps them out of common walking paths in your home.

- Set a small table or stool by the door on which to leave packages, groceries, and so forth when unlocking the door.

- Place night-lights in the bathroom and hallways.

- Make sure all railings and grab bars in the house are secure (and if the home doesn't have a properly installed grab bar in the bathtub, consider calling a qualified installer today).

LET'S TALK/REMINISCE:

- Does anything in your living environment make you feel unsafe?

- Is there anything that would help you feel safer in your home?

- What physical changes do you notice the most as you have aged?

CAREGIVER PERSONAL PRACTICE

Plan for emergencies.

Do you have an emergency escape plan if there were a fire in your own home? A fire extinguisher on each floor of the house? Don't waste time castigating yourself if you don't. Simply forgive and prepare a plan as an act of love. Add smoke and carbon monoxide detectors to your home or check that the ones you have are functioning and have fresh batteries.

 **WATERING RITUALS**

> *"Let your love be like misty rain, gentle in coming but flooding the river."*
>
> **—African proverb**

SHARED ACTIVITY:

The role of water in nature is awe inspiring. Houseplants, pets, landscapes, and loved ones all need water to survive. With your care partner, list all the watering rituals that you may engage in on a regular basis. For instance, do you drink a glass of water upon waking? Fill the cat's or dog's water bowl in the morning? Is there a certain day of the week that you water the houseplants, yard, or garden?

These acts, though routine, are indeed little acts of love, revealing a reverence for life. Be mindful as you perform your watering rituals today; be proud of engaging in these loving activities.

LET'S TALK/REMINISCE:

- Would you rather visit a pond, a lake, a river, or an ocean?
- What role did water play in your childhood?
- Was water part of your family vacations?

CAREGIVER PERSONAL PRACTICE

Water cycles.

Water is one of the key ingredients to life. Without water, all living things, including humans and plants, would cease to exist. The Earth's water cycle, which perpetually recycles water from the Earth to the atmosphere through evaporation and then back to the Earth again through precipitation, is critical to life itself. The Earth's water has been recycled for millions of years, meaning that some of the very water that you drink today, or consume through fruits and vegetables, may have been consumed by the dinosaurs or by multiple humans millennia ago. As you consume water today, give a nod to the deep connection we have to the past, present, and future through the water in our life.

Whether it's a quick trip to the grocery store, a regular visit to the physician's office, a ride to and from a house of worship, or a leisurely day out and about, the time you have together with your care partner while in the car or on the bus or train is an opportunity to be present, listen, and savor each other's company. Here are some ways you can harness the power of gratitude, empathy, forgiveness, love, and awe while on your journey.

 SEASONAL THANKS

ACTIVITY INSPIRATION/REFLECTION:

> *"The sun came up like gold through the trees and I felt like I was in heaven."*
>
> **—Harriet Tubman (1822–1913)**

SHARED ACTIVITY:

Whether it's spring flowers, the warmth of the sun, changing leaves, or the glistening snow, each season offers a multitude of treasures. While you are traveling today with your care partner, identify the signs of the current season that you both are grateful for. Can you each name five things that delight you? Use all your senses to fully take in the environment around you in this moment in time.

- What is your favorite season?
- If you could enjoy this season anywhere in the world, where would it be?
- What did you love to do when you were a child in this season?

CAREGIVER PERSONAL PRACTICE

Appreciate the process.

Just as the seasons bring about changes in the natural world around us, our own personal growth is constant as well. Think about the ways that you have grown in the past year. How has your role as a caregiver added to your growth and evolution as a human? Identify one thing that has made you proud of yourself this year.

 SPREAD KINDNESS

*"The smallest deed is better
than the greatest intention."*

—John Burroughs (1837–1921)

Letting a car merge into your lane, helping someone carry their bags onto the train—little acts of kindness to strangers like these seem minimal, but they can further perpetuate kindness and compassion in our world. On your journey today with your care partner, make a concerted effort to connect with and offer kindness to the people around you. Offer a smile to another rider on the bus or subway, or wave to pedestrians as you pass by. Discuss with your care partner all the ways you can spread kindness on your journeys.

- Who is the kindest person you know?
- How does being kind to others make you feel?
- How have people been kind to you?

Small acts of self-kindness.

Do one small deed to make yourself healthier today. It can be a short walk, spending 10 minutes in meditation, eating an extra serving of vegetables, or taking ten deep breaths—anything that will bring you to the present and make you feel good today.

* Bonus book suggestion: *Tiny Habits: The Small Changes That Change Everything*, by BJ Fogg.

BRIDGES TO SELF-FORGIVENESS

ACTIVITY INSPIRATION/REFLECTION:

"When the bridge is gone, the narrowest plank becomes precious."

—Hungarian proverb

SHARED ACTIVITY:

Everyone has something that they can forgive themselves for. Maybe you snapped at someone you love this week. Maybe you skipped the gym or forgot to call your friend when you said you would. Everyone deserves a little grace and self-forgiveness—including you. Have a conversation with your care partner about what you each would like to forgive yourselves for. And then on your drive today, use the bridge as a symbol of self-forgiveness. Some bridges are so small that they are easily missed as you cross them, while others are grand and exhilarating as you make your way from one side to the other. Identify some of the bridges in your community on your drive or while you are riding today. Go the extra distance to cross a bridge as an act of letting go—as you start on one side, think of the thing you wish to forgive. As you reach the other side, let it go.

LET'S TALK/REMINISCE:

- Are there bridges in your community that you cross often?

- What is the longest bridge you have ever crossed?

- What is something that you would like to forgive yourself for?

CAREGIVER PERSONAL PRACTICE

Bridge yoga pose.

The bridge pose in yoga increases blood flow throughout the body; provides a nice stretch for the back, arms, and legs; and has been shown to decrease stress. To try the bridge pose, start by lying on your back with your knees bent and feet hip-width apart. Place your arms alongside your body. Gently press your feet and arms into the floor and lift your midsection. Hold for several breaths and slowly return to the floor. Repeat a few more times. (Stop if anything causes pain.)

 ONE SPECIAL THING

*"Stay close to anything that
makes you glad to be alive."*

—Hafez (c. 1315–1390)

SHARED ACTIVITY:

Discuss on your drive one thing that would bring
a smile to both your faces. Perhaps it is stopping
for an ice cream or sharing a special lunch at
your favorite spot. It could just be sitting outside
together or reminiscing about a cherished memory. Discuss and decide on one thing to do together
that will induce joy today.

LET'S TALK/REMINISCE:

- What are some things that just always make
  you feel better?

- What are some things that always made you
  feel better growing up?

- Was there something that a family member or
  friend offered you as a child that still brings
  comfort to your soul whenever you think
  about it?

CAREGIVER PERSONAL PRACTICE

My "special things."

Think about what makes your days tolerable, enjoyable, even hopeful. Maybe it is a morning walk or an evening bath. Perhaps it is a small glass of red wine with dinner or hot tea before bed. It could be the sound of children playing or an occasional piece of chocolate. Whatever your "things" are, imagine them and recall them when you are feeling down. Have you lost some of these "things" in your role as a caregiver? If so, consider how to get a few, or even just one, back.

 **A DIFFERENT ROUTE**

ACTIVITY INSPIRATION/REFLECTION:

"To perceive the world differently, we must be willing to change our belief system, let the past slip away, expand our sense of now, and dissolve the fear in our minds."

—William James (1842–1910)

SHARED ACTIVITY:

We tend to get into routines and can even seem to get locked on autopilot when we are driving or riding to regular haunts. For a different perspective, try taking a different route today with your care partner. Sometimes when you are feeling overwhelmed or frustrated with a challenge that appears to have no solutions, it can help to look at the situation with fresh eyes. The solution might appear before your eyes suddenly.

LET'S TALK/REMINISCE:

- Is there something you have noticed on this route that you never noticed before?
- What are some things that you may benefit from if you see them from a new perspective?
- Who is someone who was always good at helping you see difficult situations from a different light?

CAREGIVER PERSONAL PRACTICE

A world of awe.

We've discussed how our own personal lenses influence how we interpret the world around us (see Chapter 2). Today, look at the world through the lens of awe. How does that affect your perspective?

Waiting in line, waiting for an appointment, waiting for a ride—depending on what you are waiting for, there can be feelings of boredom, anxiousness, fear, irritation, or contentment. Despite its negative connotations, the time we spend waiting can be time well spent with our care partners. You can use the time to explore the world around you, to find out more about the life of your loved one, or to enjoy a game together. Some activities may be appropriate for certain scenarios, and other activities may not be appropriate, but there is always space for gratitude, empathy, forgiveness, love, and awe.

 COUNT YOUR BLESSINGS

ACTIVITY INSPIRATION/REFLECTION:

> *"Reflect upon your current blessings—of which every person has many—not on your past misfortunes, of which all people have some."*
>
> —Charles Dickens (1812–1870)

SHARED ACTIVITY:

A game for you and your care partner to play while you wait includes a collective counting of your blessings. Start with the number one and name something that you are grateful for (perhaps the rain the night before) and then have your care partner name something for number two (such as the baby ducks you saw on the way to the appointment). Then it's back to you to come up with something for three (the perfect watermelon you picked up from the store). Keep track and see how far your counting can go. Can you get to ten? Twenty or more? You can stop your count as your schedule requires and pick the game back up throughout the day if you so choose.

LET'S TALK/REMINISCE:

- Have you counted your blessings in this way before?

- What are some of your favorite blessings from nature?

- What people are you most grateful for?

CAREGIVER PERSONAL PRACTICE

Counting breaths.

Slow counting as you breathe can help to regulate your breath. Today try the simple act of 5 x 5 breathing: Count to five as you inhale. Hold your breath for five. Exhale while counting to five. Hold for five. Repeat for a total of five cycles.

 **PURPOSEFUL REVIEW**

*"We have two ears and one mouth
so that we can listen twice as
much as we speak."*

—Epictetus (50–135)

SHARED ACTIVITY:

Waiting for physician appointments, tests (and test results), and other health-related appointments can be stress-inducing and spur anxiety. To ease nerves and to make the most of your wait time with your care partner, use it as an opportunity to review any of your care partner's concerns. Write down any questions that they wish the healthcare provider to address, and discuss how you, as their care partner, can help.

LET'S TALK/REMINISCE:

- Is anything causing you discomfort?
- What are your goals for today's appointment?
- What are the three main things that you would like to have addressed today?

 MAKE A "NOT-TO-DO" LIST

ACTIVITY INSPIRATION/REFLECTION:

"We can't all do everything."

—Virgil (70–19 BCE)

SHARED ACTIVITY:

Make not-to-do lists for today while you wait. Get out two sheets of paper, or anything on which you can write. Grab pens and, with your care partner, write down five things that you choose *not* to do today—for example, the laundry or paying bills. Then, share these lists with each other. Can you help each other *not* do what is on the lists?

- When was the last time you gave yourself permission to *not* do something?

- If you could change one thing about today, what would it be?

- What is your least favorite thing that you must do every or most days? Is there a way to reframe how you look at it to make it more positive?

CAREGIVER PERSONAL PRACTICE

Temple massage.

Holding onto anger over a perceived injustice or irritant may result in a tension headache, a dull pain in the forehead area. Relieve this tension by massaging your temples. Place both thumbs on your cheekbones, near your ears. Use your index and middle fingers to gently rub your temples (the soft indentations between the corner of your eyes and your ears). Use a small circular motion for at least 10 seconds. Repeat as desired.

💗 HOLDING HANDS

"So, we stood hand in hand like two children, and there was peace in our hearts for all the dark things that surrounded us."

—Arthur Conan Doyle (1859–1930)

SHARED ACTIVITY:

Hold hands with your care partner while you are waiting. Feel the energy and love flow from you to your care partner and back to you through your hands and fingers. Can you feel this? Take time to note whether your hands are cold or warm. Perhaps lotion on both would feel good? You could even give your care partner a gentle hand massage.

LET'S TALK/REMINISCE:

- Do you enjoy holding hands?
- How do you feel when you hold hands?
- Do you have a story about holding hands?

 WHAT WERE THEY BEFORE?

ACTIVITY INSPIRATION/REFLECTION:

> *"The power of finding beauty
> in the humblest things makes
> home happy and life lovely."*
>
> —Louisa May Alcott (1832–1888)

SHARED ACTIVITY:

To reflect on the deeper nature of the world around us can be an awe-inspiring experience. While you are waiting with your care partner, enjoy a little game of contemplating the items around you. What were they before? For instance, the cotton shirt you are wearing was once a cotton plant. The transparent glass window was once sand. A book was once a tree. Take turns pointing out something in your environment and talk about its natural origin.

LET'S TALK/REMINISCE:

- What are some of your favorite things that have been transformed from their original nature?

- What are some of your favorite things that require no transformation from their original nature?

- Are there any items that amaze you by their transformation?

CAREGIVER PERSONAL PRACTICE

Awe-maze yourself.

Spend a few minutes while you wait freewriting about an issue or experience that you are stuck on and can't get beyond. Just grab a blank sheet of paper and a pen and start writing; no thoughts or words or phrases are wrong. Freewriting helps us to explore our feelings and thoughts in a non-judgmental and loving way. This exercise can also help you improve your sense of control and give you insights into your deepest self. You might awe-maze yourself.

*"To me every hour of the light
and dark is a miracle."*

—Walt Whitman (1819–1892)

Chapter 9

Forty Micro-moments of Self-Care for Caregivers

Finding enough time or energy for self-care is a common struggle for caregivers. Each of the Positive Caregiving activities provided in the previous chapters offer you a caregiver personal practice idea to help you care for yourself as you care for your care partner.

In this chapter, we have pulled some of those ideas and supplemented them with additional ideas for simple, micro-moments of gratitude, empathy, forgiveness, love, and awe that are easy to incorporate into your daily life and can help you relax, refocus, and refresh. We've also noted many of the physical, mental, and emotional benefits of the personal practices.

As with the other content in this book, you may want to try many of them, or you may find one or two micro-moments that fit well into your schedule, lifestyle, and preferences.

- **Spot *komorebi***
  In Japanese, the word *komorebi* (koh-moh-reh-bee) is the term used to describe the sunlight as it filters through the trees. See if you can catch a moment of *komorebi* this week. Let the light wash over you.

- **Step outside into the sun**
  Take a moment to go outside and savor the warmth of the sunshine on your skin. The natural light boosts serotonin in the brain, which then helps you feel more energetic, emotionally positive, and mentally focused.

- **Look and listen for birds**
  Mother birds teach their offspring how
  to sing, just like our parents taught us how to
  speak. Seeing and hearing birds in daily life
  has been shown to help decrease stress and
  anxiety. Bring yourself to the here and now by
  patiently looking for a bird in the sky, on the
  ground, or in a tree. If you are outside, listen
  for their songs.

- **Three good things**
  Quick. Name three things you are grateful
  for right now. This small task, also known
  as the Three Good Things (TGT) exercise,
  was created by the founder of the Positive
  Psychology movement, Martin Seligman. It
  has been proven to increase happiness and
  reduce stress. Try it anytime you need a little
  pick-me-up.

- **Spot the daytime moon**
  The moon is often visible in the daytime. Take
  a moment to see if you can find it. If the sky is
  cloudy, know that above the layers of gray, the
  sun and the moon are holding Earth in place,
  just as they have for billions of years.

- **Focus all five senses**
  Let your five senses bring you to the here and
  now. At this very moment, what do you hear?
  Smell? See? Taste? Feel? Bringing yourself to
  the present on a regular basis can help you stay
  focused, boost your happiness, and counterbalance negative emotions like anger and fear.

- **Have a natural snack**
  The amazing health benefits of fresh, colorful fruits and vegetables are well documented. As you enjoy an apple, a handful of berries, or a few carrot sticks, take a moment to reflect on the natural gifts Earth has given to us in the form of delicious, nutritious foods grown with the help of the sun.

- **Identify your *merak***
  Merak (pronounced mehr-ahk) is a Serbian term describing a feeling of bliss and transcendence that comes from the pursuit of small daily pleasures, which together add up to a sense of deep joy and fulfillment. Take a moment to contemplate the *merak* in your life.

- **Color spotting**
  Stop and look around. Spot and name five yellow (choosing any specific color will work) things that you see. This simple act can help ease your mind when you are feeling overwhelmed or ruminating on negative thoughts.

- **Give a hug**
  Hugging brings you to the here and now. Embracing someone you love releases happy hormones in your body that can help reduce stress and pain, improve the immune system, lift your mood, and build stronger emotional bonds.

- **Take a deep breath**
  Take a deep breath in. Hold it. Exhale slowly. Deep breathing is one of the quickest ways to decrease stress. By taking slow, deep breaths, the body is telling the brain to relax.

- **Close your eyes**
  Close your eyes. Even for a moment. It can relax and calm the brain, help you think more clearly, improve memory recall, and boost your creativity.

- **Start the day with gratitude**
  When you wake, before you get out of bed, think of one thing that you are thankful for. When you feel gratitude, dopamine, serotonin, and oxytocin are released in the brain. These chemicals induce feelings of connection and happiness. They also help moderate your body's response to stress.

- **Say an affirmation**
  An affirmation is a positive statement that you repeat to yourself to overcome negative thinking. To create an affirmation, choose words that resonate with you and make you feel good. An affirmation can be as simple as "I can do this." Or it can be more specific to your personal situation. In conjunction with taking slow, deep breaths, repeating affirmations can lower stress and decrease troublesome rumination.

- **Turn up the tunes**
  Put on some music. Music can work miracles on the brain. Reducing stress, decreasing pain, and lessening depressive symptoms are just some of the potential benefits. Music can also improve cognitive and motor skills, and even team up with the brain to produce new neurons—the building blocks of memory-making and retrieval.

- **Massage your temples**
  Relieve tension by massaging your temples. Gently rub the area with your fingers using small circular motions. Alternate between circling clockwise and counterclockwise. Take deep breaths and close your eyes if you'd like. You might notice that focusing a little TLC on this one area helps bring a sense of stillness to the rest of the body.

- **Let out a sigh**
  A good sigh can do you good. Take a long, deep breath and let out a big sigh on the exhale. This form of breathing triggers neuropeptides in the brain that send the message to your body to relax. Sighing can also help lower your stress levels and improve your lung function.

- **Reach up**
  Reach your arms above your head and s-t-r-e-t-c-h. Stretching for 10 to 15 seconds can increase your circulation, decrease muscle

tension, and help you to relax. You can reach your hands up high while sitting down or standing up.

- **Give yourself a hug**
  Wrap your arms across the front of your torso, reaching your hands to your back, and squeeze. Like hugging others, a self-hug can reduce pain, release tension, and lower blood pressure.

- **Palm press**
  Press your palms together. Keep pressing while you take five breaths, then release. This simple pressure exercise can help you relax your muscles, calm your nerves, and build arm strength.

- **Amplify joy**

  Magnify your own joy by amplifying someone else's good news, starting with your care partner. Seek out the positive in your care partner's life and celebrate it together. When you amplify a loved one's good news, it strengthens your bond and boosts your positive feelings at the same time.

- **Count backward**
  Close your eyes and slowly count backward from 10 to 1. On each count, take a deep inhale or exhale. 10, 9, 8, 7, 6, 5, 4, 3, 2, 1. Counting up to 10 is something we can do automatically. Counting backward engages

the brain in a more challenging way, forcing you to slow down. In fact, studies show that counting backward can help calm your nerves, focus your thoughts, and reduce anxiety.

- **Review learning**
  Learning new things at any point in life builds new neuropathways and strengthens neural networks in the brain. Tonight, before you go to sleep, think about all the things that you learned today. Was there something you learned that surprised you? Reviewing what you learn can help you remember new data more efficiently and reminds you to acknowledge your continuous personal growth.

- **Reread inspiring words**
  Reading a favorite saying can provide a comforting thought before you put your head down at night or a calming way to start your day when you wake up. Write out a quote or an affirmation that resonates with you on a stiff piece of paper or index card and keep it within reach of your bed. For example, if you read in bed, you can use it as a bookmark.

- ***Hara hachi bu***
  Following Confucian wisdom, practice mindful eating by following the rule of *hara hachi bu*, which means to stop eating when 80 percent full. Try thinking *hara hachi bu* before your meals today and see how this mindfulness trick can keep your mind focused on

your food, your belly satisfied, and your body happy.

- **Foot grounding**
  Place both feet on the ground. With your shoes on or off, press your toes firmly into the earth. Feel yourself come fully to the current moment. You are here. You are alive. You are a miracle. Small studies of this form of "grounding" indicate that it may help reduce stress, pain, and inflammation.

- **Wise offerings**
  Every person has wisdom to share. Before you go to sleep tonight, take a moment to think about your own knowledge, experience, and expertise. Quietly contemplate a few ways that you could use your wisdom to help others.

- **Go to your happy place**
  If you find yourself feeling anxiety or stress bubbling up inside, close your eyes and think of one of your favorite places—somewhere you felt relaxed and one with the universe. Take a few deep breaths as you imagine yourself being there. Visualization exercises can help refocus your thoughts and calm you quickly.

- **Mini hand massage**
  Give yourself a small act of kindness with a mini hand massage. Apply lotion or cream to your skin. Take extra time to rub it in and

relax in the moment. As you enjoy this pampering, give thanks for all that your hands allow you to do.

- **Write it out**
  Writing can be a form of meditation and a practice of mindfulness. Take five minutes to write continuously about anything that comes to your mind. Pay attention to the act of writing: Feel the pen in your hand, its tip scrolling on paper. Notice the unique way you write and be grateful for the gift of your own voice. Even five minutes of freewriting (without stopping to correct errors, make changes, etc.) can improve your focus and well-being.

- **Gentle eye press**
  Applying pressure to specific parts of the body has been used for millennia in Chinese medicine to help relieve a variety of ailments, including stress and anxiety. Gently apply pressure with two fingers or your thumb to the center of each eyebrow. Take a few deep breaths and feel yourself calm.

- **Sit in silence**
  Sit in complete silence for a few minutes. Silence has a multitude of benefits for our physical and mental well-being. Sitting in silence can help lower blood pressure and may even improve sleep. It also gives you a mental break when you can reflect quietly.

- **Visualize your loved ones**
  Close your eyes and picture some of the people in your life you care deeply about and who bring you joy. This simple visualization exercise can help balance out or reduce the intensity of negative feelings like stress and anxiety.

- **Run water over your hands**
  Run warm or cool water over your hands. Let the water run down your fingers and off your fingertips. Flip your hands back and forth to let the water run slowly over the back of your hands and then your palms to calm yourself and bring you to the present quickly.

- **Find a new perspective**
  Choose a window in your home that you rarely look out of, then spend a few minutes looking through that window and take notice of the view. What are some things you have never noticed before? Contemplate whether there is something in your life that could benefit from a new perspective.

- **Savor tea**
  The act of drinking hot tea or a warm tisane (the proper name for herbal tea) is an opportunity for regaining focus. Cup your hands around your tea. Hold the cup of tea (or tisane) to your nose. Feel the warmth/steam rise to your nose. Take a deep inhale and exhale. Let your mind become fully present before taking the first sip.

- **Write and toss**
  Write a list of things that have been bothering you lately or any negative thoughts that you might have. They can be anything big or small. Once you have purged them from your mind onto the paper, crumple the paper and discard it. Research has shown that this simple act may help you to gain control over negative thinking.

- **Organize your nightstand**
  A simple measure to help calm your mind and improve your sleep is to keep your bedside table functional and clear of clutter. Take a few minutes to organize the contents of your nightstand. Throw out or store items that aren't essential to a good night's sleep. Add a small tray for a water glass. Have some tissues handy. Make sure charger cords are wound up and easily accessed. Keep several books to peruse. Add a small wastebasket near the bed to help keep the table free of waste.

- **Just one hour**
  Turn on your phone's Do Not Disturb function one hour before bedtime. Resist the urge to look at the screen until the morning. The blue light from our electronic devices, including our phones, can disrupt a restful night's sleep. Turning away from your phone for just one hour before bedtime may help you fall asleep more easily and improve attentiveness the next day.

- **Warm blanket**
  Throw a clean, dry blanket in the dryer and let it run for 5 to 10 minutes. Use the warmed blanket to give yourself a comforting gift of kindness on the couch as you watch a show, in a chair while you read, or as you lie down in bed.

The next time you think, "I just don't have time to take care of myself," refer back to this chapter and try one of these quick activities. Better yet, highlight suggestions that speak to you the most. In those moments when time feels scarce, you'll appreciate the effort you took now to make it easy for you to show yourself some love.

"Being deeply loved by someone gives you strength, while loving someone deeply gives you courage."

—Lao Tzu (~500 BCE)

Chapter 10

Ideas for Different Caregiving Scenarios

Caregiving scenarios

vary based on many factors, including your care partner's living arrangements, their needs and abilities, and whether you have assistance from others (including family, friends, and paid care professionals) in providing care.

Common caregiving scenarios include:

- sudden/new caregivers
- remote caregivers
- part-time caregivers
- full-time caregivers
- caregivers of those who are living in assisted living, memory care, or nursing homes.

Positive Caregiving was designed with all care partners, regardless of your caregiving scenario, in mind, to help you savor your days, nourish your souls, and grow in your relationships and as an individual. While using any activity listed throughout this book can be helpful, it's also true that not every activity will be a good fit in every scenario. To help you jump right to an exercise or practice that fits your particular situation, I've listed a handful of suggested activities that are good fits for each caregiving scenario that may help you get started.

If and when you are ready to start savoring the day and finding joy, below are some suggested activities focused on gratitude, empathy, forgiveness, love, and awe that are well-suited for care partners who are at the beginning of their journey.

(And if you would also like some guidance on navigating the practicalities of caregiving, I've written a free guide called *Inhale Love, Exhale Fear: Positive Caregiving's Step-by-Step Guide to the First 30 Days in Your Caregiving Journey*. This booklet can help you get organized and stay on top of your loved one's care—the medications, appointments, doctors, forms, chores, and coordination that caregiving entails. You can download it at positivecaregiving.com.)

 Gratitude

Neighbor Appreciation, pg. 50

 Empathy

Care Partner Mission Statement, pg. 72

 Forgiveness

Accepting What You Cannot Change, pg. 97

 Love

One Special Thing, pg. 172

 Awe

Ordinary Miracles, pg. 129

Caregiving for a loved one from a distance has its own unique challenges, but rest assured, it can be done and is done by millions of people every day. And there are still ample ways to incorporate gratitude, empathy, forgiveness, love, and awe into this caregiving scenario to help you and your care partner savor the days and grow in your relationship from afar. Here are some activity ideas to help get you started.

 Gratitude

Celebrate Someone's Good News, pg. 53

 Empathy

Trading Places, pg. 71

 Forgiveness

Face Fears, pg. 98

 Love

I Love You Because, pg. 109

 Awe

Memories of Awe, pg. 133

From running errands and paying bills to providing rides to appointments and helping with household chores, many loved ones provide part-time assistance to their care partners that may take a few hours to tens of hours per week. This shared time, while being of service to your care partner, is also an opportunity for joy. Below are some ideas to help savor your time together.

 Gratitude

    Reaching Out, pg. 57

 Empathy

    Spread Kindness, pg. 169

 Forgiveness

    "Done" Lists, pg. 92

 Love

    Home Adaptations, pg. 163

 Awe

    Watering Rituals, pg. 165

Some full-time care partners are spouses/partners who have lived together for many years. Others are adult children who opt to live with an older loved one full-time, whether for a short while (such as during a rehabilitation period) or more permanently (where you merge residences). These full-time caregiving scenarios offer people more time to adjust to each other's unique qualities and needs—they can also make it easy to forget the potentially wondrous opportunity that this time provides for savoring the day-to-day together. Below are some activity ideas to help keep gratitude, empathy, forgiveness, love, and awe in the mix.

 Gratitude

An Unexpected Thank-You, pg. 51

 Empathy

Moon Gazing, pg. 75

 Forgiveness

Recent Tensions, pg. 101

 Love

Bake a Family Favorite, pg. 155

 Awe

Seeds, pg. 131

From helping to manage health care and finances to providing emotional support, many caregivers find themselves in a scenario where they are supporting care partners who reside in a long-term care community, whether it is assisted living, memory care, or nursing homes. Although your time together may be limited by visiting hours, there are a lot of ways to savor the time that you do have together. Here are some activity ideas to incorporate gratitude, empathy, forgiveness, love, and awe into those visits and outings.

 Gratitude

Grateful Lists, pg. 59

 Empathy

Mosaic Magic, pg. 78

 Forgiveness

Letting Go of Regrets, pg. 94

 Love

Memory Boxes, pg. 110

 Awe

Love Without End, pg. 136

Of course, you may be experiencing multiple different caregiving scenarios—maybe your spouse is recuperating from a fall and one of your parents is in memory care, or one of your parents is showing early signs of frailty when an in-law is adjusting to life after recently losing a spouse. If this is the case for you, feel free to mix and match from the lists in these chapters to find a recipe of activities that fit your unique situation.

In addition, the micro-moments of self-care listed in Chapter 9 will be extra important for you. It may feel like all you have time for is micro-moments, but those tiny pockets of time can still be incredibly powerful for restoring you and helping you find the headspace to look for the opportunities to experience positive emotions and all the mental and physical benefits they provide.

Finding Comfort in the Bigger Picture

As a gerontologist, I am naturally immersed in the examination of the aging process and what it means to live into advanced ages—how we change biologically, psychologically, socially, and spiritually as we move through time. This gerontological lens provides me with a unique view of life because it entails acknowledging the value of being alive while honoring the changes that occur with age, and at the same time carrying the perpetual reminder that every life ends.

As a caregiver to an older loved one it is natural to experience feelings of worry, fear, even dread thinking about our loved one's challenges or them facing their own mortality. You may even have thoughts of your own mortality.

So how can we keep ourselves hopeful while helping our care partner adapt to changes and live fully—*and* with meaning—every day of their life? I believe that harnessing the power of gratitude, empathy, forgiveness, love, and awe is the answer. Keeping these emotional lenses available to ourselves is not an effort to erase or ignore the challenges in our day-to-day lives. Rather, they are ballast. They balance the negative and steady our own well-being, so that we can continue to move forward with courage and resilience. I hope that this book has encouraged you to explore these feelings and has motivated you to bring them to the center of your caregiving journey. As you and your care partner continue to adapt and grow in your life experiences, I hope that you will consciously choose to savor the day and that you will find hope in ways that are meaningful to each of you.

As you walk your caregiving path, I also hope that you will take comfort in knowing that there is an army of caregivers who, at this very moment, are on a similar path. Although caregiving may at times feel isolating, you belong to an invaluable community. You deserve to feel proud for being part of this growing, and critically important, group of humans.

Notes

1   Freedman, V. A., Cornman, J. C., & Kasper, J. D. (2021). National health and aging trends study: Trends dashboards. *NHATS Trends Dashboard*. https://micda.isr.umich.edu/research/nhattrends-dashboards/.

2   Schulz, R. & Beach, S. R. (1999). Caregiving as a risk factor for mortality: The caregiver health effects study. *JAMA, 282*(23), 2215–2219. https://doi.org/10.1001/jama.282.23.2215;

Livingston, G., Manela, M., & Katona, C. (1996). Depression and other psychiatric morbidity in carers of elderly people living at home. *BMJ, 312*, 153–156. https://doi.org/10.1136/bmj.312.7024.153;

Pinquart, M. & Sörensen, S. (2003). Differences between caregivers and noncaregivers in psychological health and physical health: A meta-analysis. *Psychology and Aging 18*(2), 250–267. https://doi.org/10.1037/0882-7974.18.2.250;

Adelman, R. D., Tmanova, L. L., Delgado, D., Dion, S., & Lachs, M. S. (2014). Caregiver burden: A clinical review. *JAMA, 311*(10), 1052–1060. https://doi.org/10.1001/jama.2014.304;

Vitaliano, P. P., Zhang, J., & Scanla, J. M. (2003). Is caregiving hazardous to one's physical health? A meta-analysis. *Psychology Bulletin 129* (6), 946–972. https://doi.org/10.1037/0033-2909.129.6.946

3   Livingston, G., Manela, M., & Katona, C. (1996).

4   Van Durme, T., Macq, J., Jeanmart, C., & Gobert, M. (2012). Tools for measuring the impact of informal caregiving of the elderly: A literature review. *International journal of nursing studies, 49*(4), 490–504. https://doi.org/10.1016/j.ijnurstu.2011.10.011

5   Zarit, S. H, Reever, K. E., & Bach-Peterson, J. (1980). Relatives of the impaired elderly: Correlates of feelings of burden. *Gerontologist 20*(6): 649–655. https://doi.org/10.1093/geront/20.6.649

6   Schulz, R. & Beach, S. R. (1999).

7   Roth, D. L., Fredman, L. & Haley, W. E. (2015). Informal caregiving and its impact on health: A reappraisal from population-based studies. *Gerontologist 55*(2), 309–319. https://doi.org/10.1093/geront/gnu177;

O'Reilly, D., Rosato, M., & Maguire, A. (2015). Caregiving reduces mortality risk for most caregivers: A census-based record linkage study. *International Journal of Epidemiology 44*(6), 1959–1969. https://doi.org/10.1093/ije/dyv172;

Brown, R. M. & Brown, S. L. (2014). Informal caregiving: A reappraisal of effects on caregivers. *Social Issues and Policy Review 8*(1), 74–102. https://doi.org/10.1111/sipr.12002

8   Cohen, C. A., Colantonio, A., & Vernich, L. (2002). Positive aspects of care-giving: Rounding out the caregiver experience. *International Journal of Geriatric Psychiatry 17*(2), 184–188. https://doi.org/10.1002/gps.561

9   O'Reilly, D. et al. (2015).

10 Fauziana, R., Sambasivam, R., Vaingankar, J. A., Abdin, E., Ong, H. L., Tan, M. E., Chong, S. A., & Subramaniam, M. (2018). Positive caregiving charac-teristics as a mediator of caregiving burden and satisfaction with life in caregivers of older adults. *Journal of geriatric psychiatry and neurology, 31*(6), 329–335. https://doi.org/10.1177/0891988718802111

11 Seligman, M. E. P. (1999) The president's address (annual report). *American Psychologist,* 54, 559–562.

12 Yeh, B. I. & Kong, I. D. (2013). The advent of lifestyle medicine. *Journal of Lifestyle Medicine, 3*(1), 1–8.

13 Villasán Rueda, A., Sánchez Cabaco, A., Mejía-Ramírez, M., Justo-Henriques, S. I., & Carvalho, J. O. (2021). Improvement of the quality of life in aging by stimulating autobiographical memory. *Journal of Clinical Medicine,* 10(14), 3168. https://doi.org/10.3390/jcm10143168

14 Reed, A. E. & Carstensen, L. L. (2012). The theory behind the age-related positivity effect. *Frontiers in Psychology* 3, 339. https://doi.org/10.3389/fpsyg.2012.00339;

You, J., Fung, H., & Isaacowitz, D.M. (2009). Age differences in dispositional optimism: A cross-cultural study. *European Journal of Ageing* 6(4), 247. https://doi.org/10.1007/s10433-009-0130-z;

Petro, N. M, Basyouni, R., & Neta, M. (2021). Positivity effect in aging: Evidence for the primacy of positive responses to emotional ambi-guity. *Neurobiology of Aging* 106, 232–240. https://doi.org/10.1016/j.neurobiolaging.2021.06.015

15 Fredrickson, B. L. (2001). The role of positive emotions in positive psychol-ogy, the broaden-and-build theory of positive emotions. *American Psycholo-gist* 56(3), 218-226. https://doi.org/10.1037//0003-066x.56.3.218

16 Butler, R. N. (1963). The life review: An interpretation of reminiscence in the aged. *Psychiatry* 26, 65–76. https://doi.org/10.1080/00332747.1963.11023339;

Hsieh, H. F. & Wang, J. J. (2003). Effect of reminiscence therapy on depres-sion in older adults: A systematic review. *International Journal of Nursing Studies* 40(4), 335-45. https://doi.org/10.1016/s0020-7489(02)00101-3;

Lazar, A., Thompson, H. & Demiris, G. (2014). A systematic review of the use of technology for reminiscence therapy. *Health Education and Behavior* 41(1 Suppl), 51S-61S. https://doi.org/10.1177/1090198114537067;

Cuevas, P., Davidson, P. M., Mejilla, J. L., & Rodney, T. W. (2020). Reminis-cence therapy for older adults with Alzheimer's disease: A literature review. *International Journal of Mental Health Nursing,* 29(3), 364–371. https://doi.org/10.1111/inm.12692

17 Westerhof, J. G. & Slatman, S. (2019). In search of the best evidence for life review therapy to reduce depressive symptoms in older adults: A

meta-analysis of randomized controlled trials. *Clinical Psychology Science and Practice 26*(4), Article e12301. https://doi.org/10.1111/cpsp.12301;

Lan, X., Xiao, H., Chen, Y., & Zhang, X. (2018). Effects of life review intervention on life satisfaction and personal meaning among older adults with frailty. *Journal of Psychosocial Nursing and Mental Health Services, 56*(7), 30–36. https://doi.org/10.3928/02793695-20180305-01;

Le, T. N. & Doukas, K. M. (2013). Making meaning of turning points in life review: Values, wisdom, and life satisfaction. *Journal of Religion, Spirituality & Aging 25*(4), 358–375. https://doi.org/10.1080/15528030.2013.765367

18 Davis, D. E., Choe, E., Meyers, J., Wade, N., Varjas, K., Gifford, A., Quinn, A., Hook, J. N., Van Tongeren, D. R., Griffin, B. J., & Worthington, E. L. (2016). Thankful for the little things: A meta-analysis of gratitude interventions. *Journal of Counseling Psychology, 63*(1), 20–31. https://doi.org/10.1037/cou0000107

19 Emmons, R. A. & McCullough, M. E. (2004). *The Psychology of Gratitude.* Oxford University Press;

Emmons, R. A. & McCullough, M. E. (2003). Counting blessings versus burdens: An experimental investigation of gratitude and subjective well-being in daily life. *Journal of Personality and Social Psychology 84*, 377–389. https://doi.org/10.1037//0022-3514.84.2.377;

Wood, A. M., Froh, J. J. & Geraghty, A.W. (2010). Gratitude and well-being: A review and theoretical integration. *Clinical Psychology Review 30*(7), 890–905. https://doi.org/10.1016/j.cpr.2010.03.005

20 Wood, A. M., Maltby, J., Gillett, R., Linley, P. A., & Joseph, S. (2008). The role of gratitude in the development of social support, stress, and depression: Two longitudinal studies. *Journal of Research in Personality, 42*(4), 854–871. https://doi.org/10.1016/j.jrp.2007.11.003;

Yu, H., Gao, X., Zhou, Y., & Zhou, X. (2018). Decomposing gratitude: Representation and integration of cognitive antecedents of gratitude in the brain. *The Journal of Neuroscience 38*(21), 4886–4898. https://doi.org/10.1523/JNEUROSCI.2944-17.2018

21 Sunding, B. A. (2015). Gratitude in long term care. *Journal of Psychology & Clinical Psychiatry 2*(4): 00084. https://doi.org/10.15406/jpcpy.2015.02.00084

22 Seligman, M. E., Steen, T. A., Park, N., & Peterson, C. (2005). Positive psychology progress: Empirical validation of interventions. *American Psychologist, 60*(5), 410–421. https://doi.org/10.1037/0003-066X.60.5.410

23 Fredrickson, B. L. (2004). The broaden-and-build theory of positive emotions. *Philosophical Transactions B, The Royal Society Publishing, London.* 359(1449), 1367–78. https://doi.org/10.1098/rstb.2004.1512

24 Sturm, V. E. et al. (2013). Heightened emotional contagion in mild cognitive impairment and Alzheimer's disease is associated with temporal lobe degeneration. *Proceedings of the National Academy of Sciences of the United States of America 110*(24), 9944-9. https://doi.org/10.1073/pnas.1301119110

25 Lamm, C., Silani, G. & Singer, T. (2015). Distinct neural networks underlying empathy for pleasant and unpleasant touch. *Cortex; a journal devoted to the*

study of the nervous system and behavior 70, 79–89. https://doi.org/10.1016/j.cortex.2015.01.021

26 Knafo, A., Zahn-Waxler, C., Van Hulle, C., Robinson, J. L., & Rhee, S. H. (2008). The developmental origins of a disposition toward empathy: Genetic and environmental contributions. *Emotion (Washington, D.C.)*, 8(6), 737–752. https://doi.org/10.1037/a0014179

27 Zahn-Wexler, C. et al. (1992). Development of concern for others. *Developmental Psychology* 28(1), 126–136.

28 Goldstein, T. R. & Winner, E. (2012). Enhancing empathy and theory of mind. *Journal of Cognition and Development.* 13(1), 19–37. https://doi.org/10.1080/15248372.2011.573514

29 Oh, J., Chopik, W. J., Konrath, S., & Grimm, K. J. (2020). Longitudinal changes in empathy across the life span in six samples of human development. *Social Psychological and Personality Science,* 11(2), 244–253. https://doi.org/10.1177/1948550619849429;

Beadle, J. N. & de la Vega, C. E. (2019). Impact of aging on empathy: review of psychological and neural mechanisms. *Frontiers in Psychiatry* 10, 331. https://doi.org/10.3389/fpsyt.2019.00331

30 Cohen, S., Schulz, M. S., Weiss, E., & Waldinger, R. J. (2012). Eye of the beholder: the individual and dyadic contributions of empathic accuracy and perceived empathic effort to relationship satisfaction. *Journal of Family Psychology : JFP : Journal of the Division of Family Psychology of the American Psychological Association (Division 43)*, 26(2), 236–245. https://doi.org/10.1037/a0027488

31 Rumble, A. C., Van Lange, P. A. M., & Parks, C. D. (2010). The benefits of empathy: When empathy may sustain cooperation in social dilemmas. *European Journal of Social Psychology,* 40(5), 856–866.

32 Riess, H. (2017). The Science of Empathy. *Journal of Patient Experience*, 4(2), 74–77. https://doi.org/10.1177/2374373517699267

33 Riess, H. (2017).

34 Cheng, S. T., Ip, I. N., & Kwok, T. (2013). Caregiver forgiveness is associated with less burden and potentially harmful behaviors. *Aging & Mental Health*, 17(8), 930–934. https://doi.org/10.1080/13607863.2013.791662

35 Lawler, K. A., Younger, J. W., Piferi, R. L., Jobe, R. L., Edmondson, K. A., & Jones, W. H. (2005). The unique effects of forgiveness on health: An exploration of pathways. *Journal of Behavioral Medicine*, 28(2), 157–167. https://doi.org/10.1007/s10865-005-3665-2

36 Kaleta, K. & Mróz, J. (2018). Forgiveness and life satisfaction across different age groups in adults. *Personality and Individual Differences* 120, 17–23. https://doi.org/10.1016/j.paid.2017.08.008

37 Friedberg, J. P., Suchday, S., & Srinivas, V.S. (2009). Relationship between forgiveness and psychological and physiological indices in cardiac patients. *International Journal of Behavioral Medicine* 16, 205–211. https://doi.org/10.1007/s12529-008-9016-2

38 Farrow, T. F., Zheng, Y., Wilkinson, I. D., Spence, S. A., Deakin, J. F., Tarrier, N., Griffiths, P. D., & Woodruff, P. W. (2001). Investigating the functional anatomy of empathy and forgiveness. *Neuroreport* 12(11), 2433–2438. https://doi.org/10.1097/00001756-200108080-00029

39 van Oyen Witvliet, C., Ludwig, T. E. & Vander Laan, K. L. (2001). Granting forgiveness or harboring grudges: Implications for emotion, physiology, and health. *Psychological Science* 12(2), 117–123. https://doi.org/10.1111/1467-9280.00320

40 Owen, A. D., Hayward, R. D., & Toussaint, L. (2011). Forgiveness and immune functioning in people living with HIV-AIDS.

41 Toussaint, L. et al. Editor choice: Let it rest: Sleep and health as positive correlates of forgiveness of others and self-forgiveness. *Psychology & Health* 35(3), 302-317. https://doi.org/10.1080/08870446.2019.1644335

42 Wade, N. G. & Tittler, M.V. (2019). Psychological interventions to promote forgiveness of others: Review of empirical evidence. In Worthington, E. L., Jr. & Wade, N .G. (Eds.) *Handbook of Forgiveness* (pp. 255–265). Routledge/Taylor & Francis Group.

43 Hayward, R. D. & Krause, N. (2013). Trajectories of change in dimensions of forgiveness among older adults and their association with religious commitment. *Mental Health, Religion & Culture* 16(6). https://doi.org/10.1080/13674676.2012.712955

44 Toussaint, L. L., Owen, A. D., & Cheadle, A. (2012) Forgive to live: Forgiveness, health, and longevity. *Journal of Behavioral Medicine* 35, 375–386. https://doi.org/10.1007/s10865-011-9362-4

45 Levy, K., Grant, P. C., Clem, K., Eadie, D. S., & Rossi, J. L. (2021). Holding onto Hurt: The Prevalence of Interpersonal Hurt and Need for Forgiveness-Focused Solutions for Hospice Family Caregivers. *Journal of Palliative Medicine*, 24(8), 1139–1146. https://doi.org/10.1089/jpm.2020.0521

46 Sternberg, R. J. & Weis, K. (Eds.) (2006). *The New Psychology of Love*. Yale University Press.

47 Heshmati, S. et al. (2017). What does it mean to feel loved: Cultural consensus and individual differences in felt love. *Journal of Social and Personal Relationships*. https://doi.org/10.1177/0265407517724600

48 Bradley, J. M. & Cafferty, T. P. (2001). Attachment among older adults: Current issues and directions for future research. *Attachment & Human Development* 3(2), 200–221. https://doi.org/10.1080/14616730126485

49 Carter, C. S. (2017). The oxytocin-vasopressin pathway in the context of love and fear. *Frontiers in Endocrinology* 8, 356; https://doi.org/10.3389/fendo.2017.00356

Carter, C. S. (2017). The role of oxytocin and vasopressin in attachment. *Psychodynamic Psychiatry* 45(4), 499517. https://doi.org/10.1521/pdps.2017.45.4.499

50 Oravecz, Z., Muth, C., & Vandekerckhove, J. (2016). Do People Agree on What Makes One Feel Loved? A Cognitive Psychometric Approach to the

Consensus on Felt Love. *PLOS One*, 11(4), e0152803. https://doi.org/10.1371/journal.pone.0152803

51 Frederickson, B. L. (2013). Chapter One—Positive Emotions Broaden and Build. *Advances in Experimental Social Psychology 47*, 1–53.

52 Silvia, P. J., Fayn, K., Nusbaum, E. C., & Beaty, R. E. (2015). Openness to experience and awe in response to nature and music: Personality and profound aesthetic experiences. *Psychology of Aesthetics, Creativity, and the Arts*, 9, 376–384.

53 Keltner, D., & Haidt, J. (2003). Approaching awe, a moral, spiritual, and aesthetic emotion. *Cognition and Emotion, 17*(2), 297–314. https://doi.org/10.1080/02699930302297

54 Keltner, D. & Haidt, J. (2003);

Shiota, M. N., Campos, B., & Keltner, D. (2003). The faces of positive emotion: Prototype displays of awe, amusement, and pride. *Annals of the New York Academy of Sciences*, 1000, 296–299. https://doi.org/10.1196/annals.1280.029;

Piff, P. K., Dietze, P., Feinberg, M., Stancato, D. M., & Keltner, D. (2015). Awe, the small self, and prosocial behavior. *Journal of Personality and Social Psychology*, 108(6), 883–899. https://doi.org/10.1037/pspi0000018;

Shiota, M. N., Keltner, D., & John, O. P. (2006). Positive emotion dispositions differentially associated with big five personality and attachment style. *The Journal of Positive Psychology 1*(2), 61–71. https://doi.org/10.1080/17439760500510833;

Shiota, M. N., Keltner, D., & Mossman, A. (2007). The nature of awe: Elicitors, appraisals, and effects on self-concept. *Cognition and Emotion*, 21:5, 944963, DOI: 10.1080/02699930600923668;

Silvia, P. J. et al. (2015), 376–384;

Stellar, J. E., John-Henderson, N., Anderson, C. L., Gordon, A. M., McNeil, G. D., & Keltner, D. (2015). Positive affect and markers of inflammation: Discrete positive emotions predict lower levels of inflammatory cytokines. *Emotion (Washington, D.C.)*, 15(2), 129–133. https://doi.org/10.1037/emo0000033

55 Piff, P. K. et al. (2015).

56 Schneider, K. J. (2009). *Awakening to Awe: Personal Stories of Profound Transformation*. Jason Aronson, Inc.

57 Konečni, V. (2011). Aesthetic trinity theory and the sublime. *Philosophy Today 55*(1), 64-73. https://doi.org/10.5840/philtoday201155162

58 Yaden, D. B., Haidt, J., Hood, R. W., Jr., Vago, D. R., & Newberg, A. B. (2017). The varieties of self-transcendent experience. *Review of General Psychology*, 21(2), 143–160. https://doi.org/10.1037/gpr0000102

59 Schneider, K. (2017). The resurgence of awe in psychology: Promise, hope, and perils. *The Humanistic Psychologist 45*(2), 103–108. https://doi.org/10.1037/hum0000060

60 Simon-Thomas, E. R., Keltner, D. J., Sauter, D., Sinicropi-Yao, L., & Abramson, A. (2009). The voice conveys specific emotions: Evidence from vocal burst displays. *Emotion (Washington, D.C.), 9*(6), 838–846. https://doi.org/10.1037/a0017810

61 Shiota, M. N., Campos, B., & Keltner, D. (2003).

62 Silvia, P. J. et al. (2015), 376–384.

63 Rudd, M., Vohs, K. D., & Aaker, J. (2012). Awe expands people's perception of time, alters decision making, and enhances well-being. *Psychological Science, 23*(10), 1130–1136. https://doi.org/10.1177/0956797612438731

64 Piff, P. K. et al. (2015).

65 Shiota, M. N., Keltner, D., & Mossman, A. (2007).

66 Anderson, C. L. et al (2015).

Index